WITHDRAWN
CEDAR MILL COMM LIBRARY
CEDAR MILL 12505 NW CORNELL RD
PORTLAND, OR 97229
(503) 644-0043

D0955390

Dressed in Dreams

Also by Tanisha C. Ford

Liberated Threads: Black Women, Style, and the
Global Politics of Soul

Dressed in Dreams

A BLACK GIRL'S LOVE LETTER TO THE POWER OF FASHION

Tanisha C. Ford

ST. MARTIN'S PRESS
NEW YORK

The names and identifying characteristics of some persons described
in this book have been changed.

DRESSED IN DREAMS. Copyright © 2019 by Tanisha C. Ford.
All rights reserved. Printed in the United States of America. For information,
address St. Martin's Press, 175 Fifth Avenue, New York, N.Y. 10010.

www.stmartins.com

Designed by Kathryn Parise
Illustrations by Veronica Miller Jamison

LIBRARY OF CONGRESS CATALOGING-IN-PUBLICATION DATA

Names: Ford, Tanisha C., author.
Title: Dressed in dreams : a black girl's love letter to the power of fashion /
Tanisha C. Ford.
Description: First edition. | New York : St. Martin's Press, [2019]
Identifiers: LCCN 2019001794| ISBN 9781250173539 (hardcover) |
ISBN 9781250173546 (ebook)
Subjects: LCSH: Clothing and dress—United States. | Fashion—United States. |
African American women—Clothing. | Blacks—Race identity—United States. |
United States—Race relations. | Ford, Tanisha C.—Clothing. | African American
college teachers—Biography.
Classification: LCC GT615 .F67 2019 | DDC 391—dc23
LC record available at https://lccn.loc.gov/2019001794

Our books may be purchased in bulk for promotional, educational, or business use.
Please contact your local bookseller or the Macmillan Corporate and
Premium Sales Department at 1-800-221-7945, extension 5442,
or by email at MacmillanSpecialMarkets@macmillan.com.

First Edition: June 2019

10 9 8 7 6 5 4 3 2 1

For Ora Dee & Bennie Lou

Contents

Dressed in Dreams

1

Dashiki

We were a dashiki family in a Dickies town. And in a small Rust Belt city like Fort Wayne, Indiana, where conformity is essential for survival, this mattered. My parents were an oddball couple—one part black militant, one part bohemian dreamer—who lived full tilt in the 1970s, and forgot to hang up their dashikis at the end of the decade. Well, to be completely honest, I've never actually seen either of them don a dashiki. But I have lived with their dashiki stories—huge, mythical stories—my entire life. And I've concluded: clothes are never just garments.

Each time we stand before our closet to pick out our clothes, we make a series of choices about how we want to appear before the world. This is just as true for people who claim not to care about clothes as it is for self-proclaimed fashionistas. It's because we recognize that the way we adorn ourselves communicates something about who we are and where we come from. And everyone has experienced the discomfort of showing up somewhere dressed like they didn't get the memo. We can think of our clothes, then, as a powerful social skin.

We assume that we know what signals or markers clothes tell us about who wears them: their race, gender, sexuality, political leanings, socioeconomic status, religion, and so forth. We're not always right, but the mere fact that we *think* we know means that we believe that clothes reflect an established cultural value system.

So when we pick out our power suit because we need to feel confident in a new environment or our "Assata Taught Me" t-shirt because we want folks to know *whose* we are as soon as we walk into the room, we're aware of the social politics of dress and are finding ways to survive and thrive within social norms, or perhaps even to transgress them.

But even though the political "stakes is high" where clothes are concerned, there is room for play. Fashion allows us to turn the street into one big drag show. Through our clothes we can do our own form of world-making, imagining possibilities beyond what our current status says is our reality. And nobody does this better than people from oppressed groups, because we know what it's like to be denied access or told something isn't for us simply because of the color of our skin or who we choose to love or because we pay with food stamps.

I've devoted my entire career to unraveling the mysteries of why we make the choices we make around what we wear on our bodies and how we style our hair. It began as a way to think through how black women incorporated fashion into their activist strategies in the civil rights and Black Power movement years. Along the way, I noticed that whenever I gave talks about that moment in history, there were people of all ages who wanted to share their dressed body stories. Folks were finding joy in telling their stories and freedom in sharing their traumas in a safe space. So that got me to thinking that there was a piece of this thing that I was missing. I realized: there's power in getting dressed that goes beyond "big P" politics. There's "little p" politics—the everyday pleasures and delights of *styling out*, the strategies we use to navigate microaggressions, how we create communities around hair and dress, the ways we call out appropriation. Our garments are archives of memories—individual and collective, material and emotional—that tell these rich, textured stories of our lives. To make it plain: our clothes make us *feel* things. All the things.

I wanted to write a book that acknowledges those everyday struggles and celebrates black innovation in fashion. We are the most creative folks, knowing how to do the most with the very least, in all the best ways. I wanted to pay homage to every Big Mama and Ma'dear who made sure that even if their kids had nothing but hand-me-downs, they would be clean. I wanted to shout out the kids who had to go to school in said ill-fitting hand-me-down jeans and turned that look into the vibrant baggy jeans trend of the 1990s. I wanted to embrace the girls who survived on a steady diet of *Vibe* and *Honey* magazines and got called "ghetto" for rocking two pairs of huge doorknocker earrings, turquoise Wet n Wild lipstick, and dookie braids, only to see white girls be praised as fashion-forward when they did it. I wanted to big-up everyone who rocked a knock-off when they couldn't afford the real designer version. I wanted to give queer and trans folk in the ballroom scene their props for innovating much of what we call hip hop fashion and beauty culture, without ever getting the credit they deserved. There's a whole black fashion ecosystem that exists because of and in spite of the mainstream fashion industry, which steals as many dreams as it inspires.

I found that while I was telling everyone else's story, I had my own story to tell about coming of age in a quirky political family in a Midwestern city that most people have never even heard of. Coming face-to-face with my own stories of getting dressed has not only turned me from researcher to subject, it's made me see that black girls in the Midwest have a fashion story to tell too.

And all of my style choices and life trials and (mis)adventures can be traced back to the dashikis that I can imagine hanging in my parents' closet. My parents. The ones who taught me how to dress and dream—and how to navigate the politics therein. I am a descendant of their *fly* style and also of the generational traumas that have fractured our family. I have taken my parents' style, flipped it, remixed it, innovating with my own looks, traditions, and dress practices as a way to keep a grasp on my humanity. It definitely hasn't been easy being a dashiki daughter. As the heir apparent to my parents' weirdness, I have learned firsthand about the emotional and social torment that came with daring to express myself differently. But my parents' dashiki dreams would also lead me on a wondrous odyssey, far from Fort Wayne's rusty sartorial trappings to some of the most glamorous, fashion-forward cities in the world. By telling my fashion story, I'm telling the story of a community and a strategy for *living*, vital to our survival, shared across generations.

My dad, Herman Ford, was born into a family of Alabama share-croppers who had fled the fields of the Jim Crow South for more lucrative livelihoods in the industrial Midwest. They were a part of the Second Great Migration, which brought a massive wave of more than 5 million African Americans from rural and urban areas of the South to settle in northern and western cities across the country after World War II. My grandmother, Ora Dee, followed her brother Ollis up to Fort Wayne in 1953. Fort Wayne—an old Revolutionary War military fort turned manufacturing epicenter that sits at the nexus of three rivers—was the second largest city in the state. No one has ever called it a black cultural mecca, but it did have a lot of jobs to offer with the Pennsylvania Railroad, General Electric, Rea Magnet Wire, Phelps Dodge, and International Harvester. My father, who made his way into the world in summer 1953, was the first of the Ford children to be born in Fort Wayne, something that made him special among his siblings. Herman was the freedom baby. He had soaked up his mother's hopes of a better life up North in the womb and come out built of potential, destined to change the family's future.

But this freedom dream would be swiftly and violently inter-rupted one bloody night in December 1957, when my grandfather murdered my grandmother with a fatal blast from a twelve-gauge shotgun before turning the weapon on himself. Instantly orphaned, the Ford children, now eight in number, were placed in the custody of an uncle and an older cousin who had also migrated up from Alabama.

There was always a shortage of food and clothes in their large, extended clan; any food that entered the house was quickly devoured by the children dressed in dingy hand-me-downs, who had grown accustomed to living on the edge of starvation. By the time my dad was old enough to fully understand the dire poverty and emotional minefield he and his siblings were living in in the wake of his parents' murder-suicide, he already had an extensive criminal jacket. He had started breaking into neighborhood houses to steal food, destroying property, racking up truancies. Crime after crime, Dad found himself trading in his hand-me-down clothes for the county-issued garb at the notorious Sol A. Wood Youth Center. "Sollywood," as they nicknamed it, was known for taking budding delinquents and turning them into hardened criminals by the time they were eighteen. The toughest teens in Fort Wayne—gang members, drug dealers, masterminds of the organized robbery syndicates—were the rebellious stars of Sollywood. Wood became my dad's second home. In his early teens, Dad would commit crimes intentionally—busting windows out of a neighbor's garage, relieving a schoolmate of his personal belongings—just so he could take up residence and enjoy three square meals a day and sleep in peace. He gladly gave up his civilian clothes for the drab Sollywood uniform.

After one time too many, a judge, tired of seeing Herman in his court, decided it was time to give the thirteen-year-old a real sentence: fifteen months at White's Institute. White's was a Quaker-run co-ed manual labor center for youth fifty miles from Fort Wayne, named after Quaker leader Josiah White. Far from a summer retreat, the work camp used Quaker religious teachings and principles of hard labor to "rehabilitate" young folks and give them skills applicable to life in the various factory towns from which they came. White's residents alternated between a week of school and a week of work. They were responsible for running everything on the multi-acre farm, from leading the lawn and construction crews to barbering all the inmates' hair. Dad was assigned to manage the dairy crew that milked the farm's forty cows. The institute offered my father the stability that he craved.

And it gave him his consciousness back. From the Quaker teachings, he took away a strong sense of responsibility and personal boundaries, things that had been numbed out of him in his uncle's house. And White's religious teachings also taught my father that black folks were equal to whites. This was not just a belief. This was knowledge—knowledge that was dangerous for a poor black boy. In a city like Fort Wayne, black folks were taught to know their place at the bottom of the social order. Whites, regardless of class, got the pick of the best housing, they got the most opportunities for advancement in the factories—even if they had fewer skills—and they lived in a city that catered every social activity to their interests. The Fort Wayne that black folks walked through was a different place. But at White's, there was nothing that made the white boys my dad worked alongside any better than him. He left White's knowing that he was just as capable of achieving as white folks were.

He returned to the house on Lewis Street, grown into muscled, sun-kissed, newly thoughtful young manhood, to find a striking girl holding court in front of the old house. Amye Glover was a mahogany-complexioned, rough-and-tumble type of girl; she sported an Afro and often donned dashikis and caftans in audacious faux African prints. The wilder the colors, the better. She was best friends with Herman's little sister Marlene. For months Amye had been hanging out at Marlene's crib, proselytizing to her friends (who weren't "conscious") about black cultural nationalism and liberation and women's rights, like she'd seen the Black Nationalist preachers do in her hometown of Cleveland. She also used her platform to tell tales of her own criminal escapades.

AMYE: Then that sucka turned around talking all that jive mess . . .

MARLENE: What'd you do, G??!!

AMYE: Sis, I told that sucka he bet not eva put his hands on my shirt again, if he knows what's good for him!!

All this loud talk wasn't a turn-on for Herman. He'd grown attached to structure, order, and work that didn't require boasting. He wasn't down with all that brash, militant rhetoric, and he walked past without acknowledging her. And that set the pattern for the remainder of high school. Amye would come around, talkin' politics and poetry and art with Marlene, and Marlene's square brother, as Amye thought of him, would pass back and forth in the background ignoring the girls.

Though she had a streetwise, hood exterior, Amye was a daughter of the black elite, and she had been groomed to join its ranks. She was bound for college—in fact, it was nonnegotiable in her family. Her father, Seaburn Glover, came from a working-class family of Pullman porters, respectable work for a black man, despite the meager wages. He'd studied history and mathematics at Florida A&M University (FAMU), where he'd also pledged Kappa Alpha Psi Fraternity, after serving in the Army during World War II. Seaburn wanted to become a teacher, like his older sister, Jeannette, a FAMU alumna who became a renowned teacher in Seminole County, Florida (and happened to be close friends and Zeta Phi Beta Sorority sisters with writer Zora Neale Hurston). But the Cleveland Board of Education made it difficult for black folks to get licensure during the age of Jim Crow, so Seaburn became a manual laborer, running the stockroom for a Jewish-owned company, making good money. His wife, Bennie Lou, came from an upwardly mobile, land-owning clan in Mississippi, boasting college degrees and Greek affiliations. Bennie Lou herself was a nurse, educated at Alcorn State University, where she also joined Zeta Phi Beta Sorority. The Glovers were the epitome of black socialites: homeowners who lived in Cleveland's respectable if still not fully integrated Mount Pleasant neighborhood. They partied with other college-educated black folks who owned fancy cocktail dresses and belonged to the major black organizations of the day—the sororities, the fraternities, the NAACP, the United Negro College Fund, Jack and Jill. The point is, Amye had all the black elite bona fides that a burgeoning socialite needed.

After a too-short lifetime of caring for others at the local hospital, Bennie Lou died of cancer. Amye was six, and she rebelled in the most dangerous ways. She developed a reputation as a serious brawler who would fight any boy or girl who dared talk smack. "Oh, your mama used to fight! All the time! She stayed in trouble," my aunt Marcia has told me on more than one occasion. By the time she was a teenager, Amye was skipping more days of school than she was attending and running with an older crowd of petty hustlers and thieves, kids who liked to steal beer and cigarettes and porterhouse steaks from the corner market.

Amye was always something of a stylish criminal, wearing hot pants and sleeveless sweater-vests, elaborate eye makeup, and false eyelashes. In her rebel gear, she was like a black Bonnie, of *Bonnie and Clyde* fame. The film, starring Faye Dunaway and Warren Beatty, was released in 1967, the heyday of Amye's crime spree. She was drawn to rebel narratives, and that admiration drew her not only to Hollywood outlaws but to the real-life Black Panthers and Black Cultural Nationalist street preachers who were highly active in Cleveland. She too would be an outlaw. That life was far more compelling than the frilly world of the Jack and Jill cotillion.

Though their class origins were starkly opposite, Mom, like Dad, underwent a major course correction as a teen. When she was fifteen her stepmother had had enough, and her parents signed the papers to have her sent to a group home two hundred miles away from Cleveland—in Fort Wayne, Indiana. She was crushed. The group home was run by a Chinese woman named Mrs. Lee and a staff of counselors and house parents. The house held twelve girls, most of whom were from other minor factory cities: Elkhart, Indiana; Grand Rapids, Michigan; and Dayton and Cincinnati, Ohio. Amye ended up staying there longer than was originally mandated. She was still getting into trouble in Fort Wayne, hanging out late, sneaking into Link's Wonderland—a black-owned nightclub with a skating rink and pool tables—and smoking reefer with her new street buddies. Mrs. Lee worried she was risking a path to prison, so she recommended to the judge who handed down the first group home sentence that Amye stay in her care at the home for the remaining three years of high school.

While Amye might have preferred to be back with her own family, Mrs. Lee's group home was far better than the alternative: girl's school. The group home afforded Amye a cultural experience that was far richer than what most black Fort Wayne folks knew. The house parents, typically middle-class white folks with college degrees, had a type of social access that even the elite black parents

Amye grew up with didn't. They introduced Amye to horseback riding at their family stables, camping and hiking at Lake Geneva (in the heart of Indiana's Amish country), French cuisine at Café Johnell, surf and turf at the seafood restaurant downtown. Through them, she gained exposure that would change her life. And mine.

One of Amye's newfound creative outlets was designing and sewing her own clothing. She already knew how to sew, but in Fort Wayne the little-used skill erupted into a passion. Her stylings became her armor. And she was particularly drawn to clothes and accessories that looked and sounded African. And nothing was more African than the dashiki.

In the Hausa language, spoken across West and Central Africa, *dan ciki* simply means "undershirt." There is a similar word in the Yoruba language: *danshiki*. To black Americans' ears, this word sounded like *dashiki*. This new word rolled off the tongue like something straight from the motherland, something special, regal even. Of course, there were many West Africans who gave black Americans the side eye when they came around asking—in broken language—to buy a shirt, like there weren't endless styles of shirts. What they were referring to was a tunic-like unisex shirt that hung to the mid-thigh or a longer women's version, both with short, wide sleeves and a deep V-neck. Over time, the dashiki did become a specific thing, highly recognized, a product of the black American imaginary, dreams of the continent made manifest in wax-printed textiles.

The key to the dashiki was purchasing the right material. Dashikis made out of cheap fabric that was only dyed on one side made you look like a shallow impostor just trying to be trendy. But if you had a dashiki made from luxe cloth that you got straight from an African boutique or, even better, directly from somewhere on the continent, you were good. Amye would scour Cleveland's fabric stores during her visits home and bring her best finds—which would have never passed as authentic to a Ghanaian or Nigerian but met the Midwestern standard just fine—back to her makeshift atelier in Fort Wayne. Dashikis were easy to make and endlessly variable. Traditionally, you use the most ornate fabric to frame the neckline, sleeves, and hem. Sometimes Amye would adhere to this style; other times her designs were more innovative. Soon she didn't even need a pattern.

No one else in Fort Wayne was really rocking dashikis. Now in Cleveland, they were popular. But once you cross over Interstate 75, the cities have a different vibe. Cleveland has a touch of the East Coast. Indiana towns feel like the up South. Not strange when you think that most of the black families in Indiana migrated from Alabama. Have you heard someone from Gary, Indiana, speak? In Fort Wayne we still have a Southern drawl too, and folksy foodways that come straight from our Alabama roots, like eating spaghetti as a side dish with a plate of hard-fried catfish and a cup of super-sweet, "red flavor" Kool-Aid. In Cleveland the black Deep South communities mingle with West Africans and folks from the black Caribbean. The Cleveland air has a little palm oil and jerk seasoning mixed in with the rust smell from its factories. This difference between Fort Wayne's and Cleveland's black populations meant that the Jo-Ann Fabrics stores in the hood in Cleveland had slightly better offerings than Fort Wayne. So that's where Amye had to go to get her dashiki fabric and keep a finger on the pulse of black liberation.

Dashikis gained popularity in the mid-60s in places like Harlem, Los Angeles, Oakland, Chicago, and Newark, New Jersey, where local newspapers reported on dashiki-wearing militants who were challenging the vestiges of Jim Crow segregation and the white supremacist ideologies that bolstered it. These journalists were the first to put the Anglicized version of *dan ciki* in print, calling the shirts worn by Stokely Carmichael, Angela Davis, and Amiri Baraka *danshiki* or *dashiki*, until dashiki stuck. Some of these revolutionary leaders got their dashikis during visits to the continent where they engaged with pan-African freedom fighters who saw the similarities between the fight against colonialism and the fight against Jim Crow. Early Peace Corps volunteers based in Africa also came home with dashikis. The shirts became a symbol of a real political commitment to freedom, one that was built upon a common ancestry, despite the fact that slavery had violently disconnected black Americans from their sisters and brothers on the continent.

The garments were also popular in cities where there were large African immigrant populations, who enriched city life with their boutiques, tailoring shops, and open-air markets. They brought over eye-catching kente, Ankara, and adinkra prints from their native countries for black American customers to caress and *ooh* and *ahh* over, as if the textiles themselves could unlock the mystery of their family's ancestral roots. And then they'd throw down some money to buy one of the dashikis hanging in the boutique or market. The really bold ones would have one tailor-made to fit, to be worn to the occasional Black History Month event or Women's Day at their Baptist or African Methodist Episcopalian church. Meanwhile, Africans living here typically still had a family member back home pick their fabric and take it and their measurements to a tailor in Accra or Lagos or Dakar, who would whip it into a beautiful something to be sent on a plane across the Atlantic with a visiting cousin or auntie.

Before long, New York–based designers such as New Breed and Palmer Brown began designing dashikis as fashionable wear.

Then mail-order companies like Eleganza began advertising dashikis in the black magazines of the day: *Sepia*, *Jet*, and *Ebony*. Patternmakers like Butterick and McCall's sold dashiki pattern kits with white cartoon models on them, putting a friendly face on the "exotic" design for the white women who would pick the patterns up at their suburban Jo-Ann Fabrics store. And seemingly overnight, a style of shirt that was just as common to Ghanaians, Nigerians, and Senegalese as blue jeans are to Americans became exceptional and sacred and deeply political for African Americans. As the dashiki grew in popularity, particularly among people who had never seen them worn in their cultural context, specificities—like which ethnic groups wore which prints and what social occasion a particular style of dashiki should be worn at—were lost. The point was simply to *own* one if you wanted to be conscious, hep, on trend, in vogue.

Amye was like a pioneer of the dashiki diaspora, bringing the radical black consciousness it represented to fashion-challenged Fort Wayne. She never really had access to authentic West African wax prints, so instead she used zebra and other animal prints and multicolored graphic material. Her dashikis were of an imagined Africa variety, the thing a person creates from their dreams of what it would be like to walk the streets of the motherland. Folks in Fort Wayne didn't know no better anyway. If Amye G., the girl from big-city Cleveland, said that's what a dashiki looked like, who was gonna check her? But very few of her peers in Fort Wayne dared wear a dashiki.

See, in a place like Fort Wayne, people learn early that the goal is to keep your head down and do your work. You punch in at a certain time, you punch out at a certain time. Push the button, lower the lever, raise the lever. People do this work repeatedly, for hours, every day, for years. Factory work does not lend itself to self-expression. Factory attire is more concerned with safety and practicality than style. Many of the folks who worked in factories in Fort Wayne had to wear coveralls to protect them from heat, or hooded sweatshirts to keep them warm in refrigerated spaces. Others wore t-shirts with durable jeans such as Dickies or construction pants by Carhartt to balance the needs of temperature control and safety.

When everyone's life is structured around the near-psychological necessity of fitting the factory mold, the whole culture of the city starts to have that vibe. Conformity. By the time it was safe for Fort Wayne black folks to publicly register the fact that an entire Black Is Beautiful movement had in fact happened, most of the freedom fighters of the 60s had either been gunned down by law enforcement, imprisoned for life, or had departed in self-imposed exile to places like Cuba and Algeria.

Amye was, in the late 60s, strutting around in her dashikis, looking like anything but a person who was preparing for a life of conformity in somebody's factory. After graduation, she headed down to Indiana University in Bloomington on a newly established minority scholarship. Later on she would talk with fondness about how she joined the same sorority as her mother and her beloved aunt Jeannette—not that she would ever commit to joining the alumni chapter. But college, with all its prerequisite courses, moved too slow for a young woman who needed constant stimulation. So she dropped out after two years and eventually returned to Fort Wayne to work for Mrs. Lee as the director of the group home where she used to live.

Herman, meanwhile, did a stint in the Army. Anticipating the draft, he had dropped out of high school a year early and earned his GED while in the military, stationed at a base near Fairbanks, Alaska, during the Vietnam War years, where he had lots and lots of time to read. The protests surrounding the war and battles for free speech, led by young people his age, politicized Herman in ways he had never been before. When he returned to Fort Wayne in the early 70s, he was in the process of becoming the New Left–leaning, voraciously educated, and upwardly mobile man that I eventually grew up with. He got himself a job at the Phelps Dodge plant and used his GI Bill benefits to enroll in an associate's degree program in business management at a nearby community college. In his off time, he would devour the classics to expand his vocabulary: *Moby-Dick*, *The Adventures of Tom Sawyer*, and W. E. B. Du Bois's *The Souls of Black Folk*. He read the newspaper religiously. Because this is the dad I grew up with, until he told me the story of his childhood, it never occurred to me that he wouldn't have been a stellar student, that with no one looking for potential in a poor black boy, his life could so easily have petered out in prison before anyone noticed his intelligence. But now he was a self-made intellectual, capable, ambitious, and confident. Always a natural athlete, he chose to take up an activity that many of the folks he grew up with thought of as a "white folks' sport": tennis. And that's how Mom and Dad finally got together. Sort of.

One day in summer 1975, Amye was visiting with her soul sister Marlene, talking about art and fashion and everything radical, like they did. Dad strolled into the house on that sweltering July day in a sweat-stained t-shirt and shorts, rippling muscles from head to toe, tennis racquet in hand. And Amye blurted out: "I play tennis too." It was clear during their first rendezvous at the park tennis court that she actually had no clue, but Dad enjoyed looking at her long, shapely legs in a tennis skirt. And after a decade of despising one another, Herman and Amye started vibing off each other's competitive energy and sense of adventure. Here were two former delinquents who had been on a fast track to prison just years earlier, now upwardly mobile by their town's standards and lobbing a tennis ball back and forth.

They bonded over their shared vision of not wanting to be a typical Fort Wayne black person. Herman had his eye on a managerial position—which had been unheard of for a black man in the 1960s—that is, if he couldn't fulfill his vision of getting out of the factory altogether. Amye shared that she wanted to finish her bachelor's degree and continue to work somewhere in the juvenile justice system. Their dashiki love affair in the land of Dickies was now a thing.

A few years ago, I found a handful of photographs from my parents' 1977 wedding in a thin white photo album resting under my dad's entertainment center. I was flush with emotion seeing those two, young and stylish and radiating love on their special day. Amye stands beside Herman, her father, and her baby sister Marcia, her sole bridesmaid, in a bohemian-esque wedding gown she sewed from a *Vogue* pattern. The dress is white, a backless, floor-length, A-line number made out of jersey knit and embellished with a very 70s lace overlay bib that hung down the front. In true Amye fashion, this dress was unconventional and risqué (the back dipped all the way to the dimples just above her derrière!). Herman is wearing a white tuxedo with a pale blue bow tie and cummerbund matching Marcia's dress, which Amye also made. They were married under the pear trees in the backyard of the house Herman and Marlene were raised in, the same house where Amye used to hold court after school.

I was born two years later, in 1979, instantly swaddled in my parents' dashiki love. I was far from the brown baby that Mom had dreamed of. I was almost ghostly pale and had "funny colored" eyes, eyes even lighter than my father's amber browns. But she vowed to love me still and was committed to making me love my own blackness (which she secretly prayed would eventually show up in my skin tone), even more. Dad was just pissed that I wasn't a boy, but he was proud that he had found a black woman who shared his vision for a life that he couldn't even have dreamed of when he was a scrappy kid, and proud to raise a child who would grow up in that shared vision. I didn't realize it until I was much older, but my parents never raised me to think I was pretty or to even be concerned with such things. I can't even think of a time where either of them said "You look so pretty." Beautiful, yes, but in that Black Power, Black Is Beautiful kind of way. I was to be tough, confident, brilliant, fierce, tenacious. A black girl-child warrior, strong enough to survive in a heartless America. I would be their dashiki dream in the way my dad had been his mother's freedom dream.

It was the girls in the group home that Mom was still running who picked out my name: Tanisha. Amye hated her white girl name, especially in the Black Power years—when people were legally shedding their Anglicized, or white, given names for "African" ones— and wanted her daughter, born in the waning years of the movement, to have a blackity-black name. And Tanisha was definitely that. Some dashiki folks were giving their kids names that came straight from Arabic, Igbo, Yoruba, Ashanti, and Swahili name books. Other kids were given these hybrid names—somewhere between African and made up, like Tanisha, Lakisha, Quanisha, Tamika, and Shanika. In the 80s and 90s, these names were read as "hood" names—used in every biting joke about "welfare queens" living in public housing in cities like East St. Louis, Pittsburgh, or Buffalo with multiple baby daddies. But in the 1970s, if you gave your daughter an -isha or -ika name, you wanted her to stand out with pride. Middle-class black families, so bound up in the anxiety of respectability politics, didn't think such names were acceptable. Would a law firm hire a black woman named Latisha? Parents like mine had much more radical concerns. Like the dashiki and the Afro, an -isha name showed that you were *proudly* black.

This naming fad has never seen a resurgence—to the point that if you meet a woman named Kanisha or Lakisha or Shanisha you can bet that she was born between 1975 and 1985. (Either that or she's from South Asia, where -isha names are traditional Hindu names. In fact, *Tanisha* means "ambition" in Sanskrit.) For us, these names are black phonetic archives of the 1970s. Mom was just honored to have the girls who were coming up in the very group home that changed her life, and whose lives she now guided, name her daughter. They picked Tanisha because it sounded like the North African country Tunisia. There are versions of the name Tanisha in both Arabic and Hausa, the Afro-Asiatic language the word *dashiki* is derived from. And in hip hop, the Afro-Asiatics are revered as the original black people. Whether the girls realized it or not, by name, I am a daughter of the diaspora, a Black Power remix.

By the early 80s, Mom and Dad had put their professional plans into action. They had navigated a rocky path on the way to achieving those employment dreams, often working multiple odd jobs—cleaning hotel rooms, bartending, and installing roofs—to make ends meet. Finally, Mom joined the Fort Wayne Police Department, sworn into the most racially diverse class of officers the city had ever seen. A job on the force came with a handsome salary and health insurance, plus a certain degree of power and prestige. Dad had earned his associate's degree in business management and was working on another in marketing (he'd eventually go on to earn a bachelor's degree in business management). One of Mom's close friends on the force, who I grew up calling "Aunt Brenda," helped my father secure a job in Mayor Wynn Moses's administration, which was looking to shake things up and address the problems of the south side of town. So Dad got to leave the factory. He traded his Dickies for a suit and tie. The new job didn't pay any more than his fairly cushy Phelps Dodge position had, but it came with a great deal of visibility and prestige, and a clunky title: Manager of Community Development and Planning.

My parents had ascended into what passed for the black middle class in our town. But here's the thing about being middle class in Fort Wayne: all it really is, is the factory managers. Most black folks who made more than $20,000—what people considered to be the floor income for middle class in those days—didn't have more than a high school education. It was quite possible to make a decent living even if you never finished high school. There weren't any true old-money blacks who summered in Martha's Vineyard or Sag Harbor or Idlewild, Michigan (or anywhere, really). Black doctors and lawyers from Fort Wayne rarely returned to the city after they left for college, so we didn't have a large black professional class. We weren't a corporate town, so there wasn't a black executive constituency. Factory workers and factory managers. That's what we were known for producing. The middle class, such as it was, could mostly be found at soirees at Aunt Brenda's house. That's where I got to know who was who in this little world—the school principals and hospital administrators and police deputies and factory managers who sank their ambition into their children by putting them in Jack and Jill.

We settled into a white, trilevel house with burnt orange shutters on Devonshire Drive, right around the corner from Aunt Brenda, in the then integrated, "upscale" Village Woods neighborhood on the southeast side of town. By the time I was in elementary school, Village Woods had been transformed. Many of the white folks had moved farther east. The area was now predominantly black; the neighborhood where the black factory managers and educators relocated their families once their paychecks started getting a little fat. And now the schools in the area were more than 90 percent black.

Even though my parents had arrived, neither of them was fully comfortable in this middle-class world. Dad disliked Aunt Brenda's parties and preferred to stay home with his books and the record collection and tech toys he could now afford. Mom loved the social aspect of the parties, but having grown up "in the life," it didn't impress her, and she could dish out some serious critiques of capitalism and the black bourgeoisie. See, for my parents, the dashiki wasn't simply about fashion. It was politics, a way of being, seeing, and experiencing the world. My parents' dashiki-draped take on gender, sexuality, race, and class made them weird—admired, envied—in our factory town, where most everyone else had been fitted for standard-issue Dickies work pants. "We were oddballs, I'm telling you! Ask any of my siblings. Having your mother helped a great deal. We were joined at the hip, heading in the right direction," Dad recently told me. My parents' attitudes, their words, the way they moved in the world were just as provocative and eye-catching and unmistakable as the ornate shirts constructed from the liveliest of West African textiles.

We dashiki Fords straddled this new Village Woods world and the poor East Central neighborhood that had brought my parents together. Now again, this being a small Midwestern town, there wasn't really much of a separation between these two worlds. Traveling across town in Fort Wayne took no more than fifteen minutes. And even if you were part of this black elite, you still lived on the same south side of town as all the other black folks. So, there was a real intimacy between the working poor, working, and middle classes of black folk, thanks to the city's long history of racial segregation, redlining, and restrictive covenants. There were a couple of parochial school exceptions, but for the most part, even if your parents were well-off, you went to public school with the same hoodlums your parents disdained, and you dated those same hoodlums, and you spoke the same slang, and you attended the same parties. Not to mention, most of the black folks who had made it had siblings who had not. So it was not at all uncommon to be making bank, by our standards, and have a fancy house and a fancy life, and have a close relative who was strung out on drugs or homeless living nearby.

Where middle class–ness began and ended was a difficult thing to pin down really. So it was the material things—like clothes, cars, and window shutters—that gave people security in their identity as having moved up. And because of the close proximity of the classes and often-tenuous family bonds, everybody knew exactly what everybody else had. In fact, that's what sparked the phrase "Don't let them folks see what you got!," which every black middle-class kid in Fort Wayne grew up hearing. For our parents, if folks know what "you got," they are likely to steal it or, even worse, be jealous. But it was an empty admonishment. Conspicuous consumption was the name of the game.

So clothing was a huge part of performing your identity. The goal was to display quantity and access to whatever was right on trend. Being ahead of the trend was scary, being behind the trend meant you were lacking. Being right on trend was where the status was. The goal was to look just like everyone in the magazines and music videos. The media when I was growing up was chronicling the explosion of hip hop, and hip hop culture did transform what being on trend meant for a Dickies town. But still, innovation always happened outside, and then we *cautiously* copied.

Unless you were Amye and Herman Ford's daughter. To be the child of dashiki dreams meant that you'd have a different relationship to clothing than your peers. I would grow up with the financial access necessary to *be* on trend and parents who supported me being as stylish and proud as possible. And I grew up with a rarer kind of access, the kind that came from having parents who were creative and political. I relished every story I could ear hustle about their past lives as young rebels, before me, and every lyric to every soul album my dad played for me on his crackly record player. And that nonconformist mindset I picked up from them showed me that

I should cast aside trends altogether and create my own brand of cool. My parents didn't try to force me to dress according to my gender or some notion of respectability. But I grew up in the suffocating confines of a factory town that always seemed to micromanage my dreams. This was the life that had been set for me: to be a weirdo in a conformist space. And I'd spend most of my young life trying to break away.

Leather Jacket

an I try it on?" I asked in excited anticipation. I was around eight years old. It was my first trip to Wilsons Leather in the mall. Moments before, the clerk had disappeared into the back before reemerging with a black Victorian-style leather jacket wrapped in a clear plastic bag with a long layaway ticket dangling from it. It was collarless, with slightly puffed sleeves, classic Victorian seaming, and a single hidden snap that hugged tight right above a flare of leather, giving the jacket a dainty peplum waist. He carefully slipped the jacket off the hanger in a manner that made the transaction seem even fancier and more important. Mom gracefully turned her back, and he slid it over her athletic shoulders. She walked over to the three-way mirror, modeling it a bit, fastening and unfastening the snap, swiveling this way and that, cocking her head, checking the angles. She looked Grace Jones–chic with the black leather jacket over her black-and-gold knee-length sheath dress, her hair shaved all over with a shock of long, layered curls on top. I absorbed her with my eyes, appreciating my mother's unique beauty.

Mom always let me try on her clothes and hats and pumps and costume jewelry when I asked. It made us feel special and connected. I think she was starting a ritual that she wished she'd had with her mother, who had died years before she even hit puberty. She slipped the jacket off and gave it back to the clerk, who almost instantly was holding it open for me. I raised my bony arms, and he slipped the jacket over my shoulders. I walked over to the mirror, mimicking what I'd seen Mom do moments before. I turned this way. I turned that way. I hugged it tight. I flared it open. The sleeves hung well past my thin wrists and the shape sagged as it tried to find the contours of my prepubescent frame. It felt very special to walk into this fashion paradise and have attentive clerks help me try on pieces of expensive leather. I wasn't big enough yet to wear this jacket without drowning in it, but I was 100 percent behind Mom's desire to add it to her growing collection.

Going into Wilsons was a black girl rite of passage. Wilsons was a popular chain retailer quickly proliferating across Middle America. They were democratizing the leather game; their layaway plan was perfect for the kind of person who had some disposable income but not enough to drop $200 to $300 up front. The store appealed largely to the twenty- and thirtysomething crowd. Of course, Wilsons' quality wasn't as good as some of the more exclusive boutiques Mom preferred, but the price points were attractive, and she was less likely to be racially profiled in Wilsons than in some high-end shop.

On the day of my first Wilsons excursion, we'd gone to our tambourine-shaking church and then driven to the mall. I was excited, but I strolled casually to match Mom's demeanor as we walked into the store. The strong outdoorsy smell of raw animal hide laced with chemicals smacked me as soon as I stepped inside the door. It was like a herd of cattle had exhaled at the same time. My mother's leather didn't smell like this, it smelled like her: hints of cocoa butter, Chanel No. 5, and flesh, the pores soaking up her essence and energy. This new leather smell made me light-headed and a bit disoriented. But then my eyes focused on the wall-to-wall racks of leather and suede jackets and handbags and wallets. This was like being in the middle of a geodesic dome of possibilities, dreams in all directions.

I walked through the store with my hand extended, like I did at home in Mom's closet, and ran it across a row of buttery-soft caramel-colored jackets. An ache of desire formed in my stomach. Leather is a curious thing to a young child. Mystical even. At home, I'd run my Dorito-stained little hands across all of Mom's different colored skirts and pants and jackets as I walked down the length of the space. Leather had a texture that I couldn't quite name. In the winter, when the heat was on blast in our house, Mom's jackets felt warm and almost clammy to the touch. In the summer, I could feel the cold of their stiff skins under my touch as the air conditioner kept the room a chilly 70 degrees. It was the only thing in her closet that felt differently depending on the temperature. Mom must have explained eventually that it was because her coats and jackets and skirts were made out of animal skin. That made me even more confused—how did a black-and-white cow produce a pink skirt? Wilsons knew just how to hook a person's instinctive carnal attraction to leather. I wanted everything in the store.

The clerk was telling Mom, "Leather is tough, but it also requires care in order to protect your investment." As I listened to him, that haunting curiosity I'd been feeling as I pondered the textures in Mom's closet finally settled down and blossomed into sense. I got it—leather's lure. I am not sure quite how tiny Tanisha would have phrased it, but I was realizing that deep in our animal brain we must feel a sense of familiarity and connection with this texture. Though it's been chemically treated and dyed and polished we can still feel its realness, its earthiness. It's a skin that breathes like our own skin. It changes in smell and texture and shape and color as it ages. Leather is more like us than any other thing we wear.

This day was a revelation. And the salesman had a compelling pitch. I was ready to gather up the coins in my treasured pale pink piggy bank to help Mom buy the lotions and sprays the clerk was hawking so she could protect her expensive investment. But she declined—she was a veteran and already knew the drill. Instead, she unfolded her neatly creased layaway receipt and handed it to the store clerk. She had "put some money on it" the last time she was in the store, and now we were here to pick up her new statement piece.

When we got home from Wilsons, I grabbed one of Mom's old photo albums down off the shelf, wanting to see the leather-maven college version of my mother—the her before there was a me. I sat on our black floral-printed sofa and traced the faces of her and her friends with my fingers, peeling back the protective cellophane cocoon covering the pictures, hearing that familiar ripping sound caused by the cellophane leaving the sticky surface to which the photos were affixed. I touched my fingers to the sticky, leaving behind a bit of my own DNA and taking with me a bit of the epoxy with each touch, feeling my skin stick and then peel away. I took one of the photographs by its corner and lifted it slowly and carefully. There she was with her big Afro and leather pants in one photo and in bell-bottoms so wide that they called them elephant pants in another. How bright and bold was her world then, when she was an independent college woman, decked out in all of the styles of the early 70s.

Mom's leather collection had started back in her raucous college days. Back then, it was all "Black Is Beautiful" and "Women Unite!," and leather was a major part of that revolutionary style zeitgeist. For my mom, the seed of the collection was a black leather vest and matching leather pants that she'd purchased impulsively with her university work-study stipend. She liked vests—they were a unisex garment that she knew she could tailor. She modified this one to hug her torso tight and create a waistline that looked good matched with the slim-fitting pair of leather pants. And she could mix and match these pieces with other pieces in her closet.

She didn't start with a jacket, because she knew that symbolism was nothing to play with. Black leather, especially in the form of a jacket, was *the* symbol of radical protest at that point. To put on the specific black leather jacket of the Black Panther Party for

Self-Defense meant that you were willing to lay down your life for the movement. Mom told me as much during one of our recent conversations. The FBI and local police were gunning down Panther members or imprisoning them for life. Young militants like Mom respected their sacrifice too much to wear their jacket—which looked similar to a German M15 military coat, with its single row of large buttons and two big pockets near the bottom—just as a *look*. It was more than that.

White feminists, too, were wearing black leather jackets in the 1970s. Theirs were more of the motorcycle, punk rock variety with zippers. Their point was to mess with the gender binary by adopting a style most typically associated with the hypermasculinity and reckless abandon of white biker culture. While Mom considered herself a feminist, that style of jacket was a little too masculine for her aesthetic. Her leather vest and pants combo let her find that sweet spot between feminine and masculine, rebel and respectable.

Leather jackets were new as a status symbol for my mom's generation, the new power suit. In real life, the Black Panthers had set the association between leather jackets and rebellious black cool, and that became part of the popular imagination, with jackets showing up on fictional crime fighters like John Shaft and Foxy Brown. Every black teen and young adult wanted to be dipped in leather! Even *Essence* magazine was instructing black college women in its annual August "Campus Issue" to buy secondhand leather and fur at thrift stores in order to be on trend on a budget.

These young folks believed that challenging the suburban ideals and obsession with respectability that had shaped the aspirations of their parents' generation was the route to freedom and power—individual or communal. My grandfather loved a well-crafted pair of leather dress shoes and leather wallets and belts, but it would never make sense to him to don a leather jacket. For this World War II veteran, leather jackets were military wear; they weren't recreational. My grandparents were married and raising children and steeped in black society life by the time that whole James Dean *Rebel Without a Cause* and Jack Kerouac Beat Generation (and the *On The Road*–inspired leather bomber jacket) thing happened. Something about the way young folks were wearing expensive leather goods seemed ostentatious to my grandfather. It drew too much attention to the wearer. Being too flashy in the 1930s and 40s, when he was coming of age, could be a death sentence. But here was his daughter, my mother, one of the flashiest dressers on her campus.

Now, back in our 1980s living room, I looked up from my perch on the couch at the woman who stood before me, and to my little eyes she was like a different person than the stylish young radical in the photo I was holding. Like most little kids, I had a hard time seeing just how cool my mom still was. The light in her eyes in the pictures had been dimmed a bit by the stresses of motherhood, marriage, and career. But I see now how in her careful way of dressing she was able to maintain some sense of herself even as her time was absorbed in caring for me and my father. The neat stack of *Ebony* and *Essence* magazines under the coffee table weren't mere decoration. Through them she could be in conversation with black women across the country.

A few years before my rite of passage at Wilsons, I began adventuring into my mother's closet. I'd creep up the stairs to the top floor of our Cape Cod–style house, all one big open-floor plan under the sloped ceilings created by the pointed roof. This was my parents' domain. There was my dad's space on the left, white walls with jade trim and a giant fuzzy rug that I loved to rub my bare feet against and all his books and office stuff. But I'd go straight for the jade-painted, white-trimmed bedroom half, with their big king-size waterbed . . . and the closet. The closet ran the full length of the house, one long line of garment after garment dangling from a rod attached to the slanted ceiling. Mom had everything you could ever want or imagine hanging from that rod, and in this big, open room, it was never shut away. I was so little I could burrow down under the clothes and the angle of the roof, the denim and leather and linen and rayon and cotton and chiffon creating their own magic corridor for me, and I'd make my way down it, exploring, discovering. She had high-waisted, pleated, and skintight leather pants, leather mini- and pencil skirts in every color of the rainbow: black, purple, teal, white, red. And leather jackets in every cut and silhouette: peplum, trench, and the full-length black leather coat she bought after seeing rapper Kool Moe Dee wear one in his "Wild, Wild West" video.

I had enough worldliness to know that leather was something of a luxury item in Fort Wayne. My mother's leather-clad sense of style set her apart from most of the other moms at school. They stuck to staid cotton and wool knit shirts in colors as bland as my morning oatmeal. My mom was edgy, colorful, like a bowl of Trix. She never liked the clothes that everyone else was wearing. Amye considered herself a member of the style elite in our little factory town. In my younger years, I cleaved to my mother, wanting everything of hers, wanting to look like her and dress like her. And every chance I got, I played dress up in her closet.

All of the most beautiful and stylish women my mom knew—my mom's baby sister, Marcia; my uncle's wife, Pam; my mom's friend Joyce and her sister Tish—loved leather. Now, some of the practical-minded folks in Fort Wayne had basic leather jackets to keep them warm in winter. But the eye-catching rainbow of coats and skirts and pants that my mom and her fashion-forward friends wore didn't seem warm or practical at all. They wore leather because it looked expensive, opulent, and luxurious, and because it was hard to find in the early 1980s.

For black folks, luxury textiles like leather and fur were immediate status symbols. One Christmas, my dad's brother Percy and his wife, Pam, rolled up to the low-key family dinner wearing matching full-length fur coats. Us kids' jaws dropped. Head-to-toe fur meant *rich* in our eyes. Only celebrities or old-money white folks on TV shows—like *Dynasty* and *All My Children*—wore fur. Of course, my aunt and uncle weren't actually wealthy. No one black in Fort Wayne was *really* wealthy. But they had all the cool rich-person bling, all the *stuff* that you could see and admire, and that's all that mattered. It was the same with Aunt Brenda and her fancy painted shutters and crazy cars. You saw Percy and Pam in their Christmas finery, that told you they had the *access* to buy a fur coat. To be able to find a store that sold a fur coat, walk into that store, not be shamed out of it or made to feel like you were coming into the store to steal, and then have enough disposable income to drop the money was a big deal. The folks making and selling luxury goods were not looking for customers among poor and working-class black folks. So we didn't have automatic access to that kind of shopping, and that's why access mattered so much. But just because something wasn't marketed toward us didn't mean we didn't want it. We wanted fur and leather and we wanted to wear it in the most ostentatious ways possible. Teenage girls like my older cousins would either "borrow" (as in steal) a coat or hook up with some drug dealer type who footed the bill.

Leather was a bit easier to come by than fur, but the right piece still gave you that exclusive feel. "That was the shit back in the day," Mom told me. "To have the leather, two or three pieces. That was the shit. And not everybody could afford it. It wasn't that anybody *said* it, you just *knew* it because you didn't see everybody in it." And that kind of sums up my mom's whole approach when she's trend-hunting.

All of my favorite celebrities looked fascinating in their unique leather styles too. Rappers Salt-N-Pepa had colorful leather S-N-P baseball jackets designed by Harlem legend Dapper Dan. Singer Vanessa Williams, the epitome of black feminine glamour, sported a sexy black leather shrug in her "The Right Stuff" video. Mom was super good at the Victorian-inspired extravaganza of leather and lace and black rocker charisma that you saw on-screen on Sheila E. and Prince. She had what it took to bring it to life on the streets of drab Fort Wayne, which made her even more magical.

While my mom was a self-assured fashion star, I was draped in my own insecurities by the time I was in second grade. Among girls my age, it was clear to everyone that light-skinned or "mixed" girls with long hair were *so* pretty. Me, with my short, "nappy" sandy-brown locks, reddish-brown skin, and fiery hazel-green eyes, I was, well, maybe, *debatably* pretty. My classmates teased me and called me "*Catrina*" on account of my funny eye color. Suddenly, when I'd look at myself in the mirror, I could see doubt in the eyes of the girl staring back at me, doubt where there previously hadn't been. But my mother, with her deep mahogany skin and decidedly short hair, was always so confident and didn't take no mess from nobody. I wanted to be like her, to possess even a sliver of her confidence.

So when I slipped into her closet, I could channel her energy. Her things were like talismans that held her confidence and beauty. One time, I shimmied her black leather pencil skirt up over my nonexistent hips. It dragged the ground, forcing me to fold the waistline several times to make it stay. I pulled the black Victorian jacket from Wilsons down off its thick hanger and put it on. I didn't yet see myself as a freedom fighter in leather—all that would come later—but I was having all kinds of feelings. It is the fundamental desire of a little girl developing a consciousness in the world: the desire to be grown, to make my own choices, to feel an unapologetic, unburdened sense of self. I tried on a pair of Mom's Connie pumps—she had a pair in every color of the crayon box. I took one of her pirate trove of clip-on shoe brooches and added it to the top of the shoe the way I'd seen Mom do countless times as she got ready for church on Sunday. The brooches, she once told me, gave her limitless mix-and-match styling options. Limitless! I balled up my fist like I was holding an imaginary microphone and began singing "*Do you wanna ride in my Mercedes, boy?*," imitating Pebbles, my favorite singer at the time. I might not ever be light skinned like Pebbles or have long, flowing honey-blond locks like hers, but in my mom's black leather ensemble, I could channel her Mercedes-level glamour.

Over the years, the world I knew and understood kept getting bigger and bigger, and so did Mom's closet. I could mark my own growth by the size of that thing. It was always "her" closet, even when she and my father shared it. When my parents were first beginning their careers, the closet space was small, humble. My father's belongings were pushed farther and farther to the side as their career successes allowed Mom to conquer more and more territory with the exotic baubles and fine textiles she won from faraway lands such as Nashville, Atlanta, and Los Angeles. Finally, just as Dad had been pushed out of the closet, he no longer occupied the central space in Mom's heart either. They got a divorce, and Dad moved out of our house and into a shabby upstairs apartment in another school district. And soon after, Mom and I would abandon the house with the jade walls and magic closet for a characterless apartment in a low-income complex. And in Dad's absence, no longer having a husband to offer commentary on her spending habits, Mom expanded her wardrobe even more, taking up closets in other parts of the apartment. She even converted another room into a walk-in closet of sorts.

By the time I was a fifth grader, Mom had amassed more than a hundred pairs of shoes, a dozen leather jackets, and countless other sundries. I was becoming greedier; I would make off with one of the amulets of her power and hide it, like a stealthy cat burglar. I figured I couldn't take the big items because she'd surely notice their absence, but I could steal something small, like a pair of earrings. But no matter how crafty I was, Mom always noticed when her things were gone. The woman had so much stuff, yet it was almost like she was Mister from *The Color Purple*, who threatened Miss Celie with a beating if she ever messed with his mailbox because he'd know if it'd been tampered with. She always knew!

On a solo mission into the closet, I could sit down and just wallow in my desire, letting the air fill up thick with my dreams. Each piece I caressed in private told me a story. The elegant leather blazer told me how it would feel to be heading into work in the middle of my big important career. The bright-colored body dress was a prophecy about the grown-up friends I'd meet up with to eat fabulous-sounding foods like chimichangas and margaritas (like my mom and her girls did every other Friday when they went to their favorite Mexican restaurant that was just far enough outside of the hood that it was slightly upscale). Tottering on the highest heels I could find, I'd spin myself through the romances I'd have with my favorite Hollywood stars, like Eddie Murphy and Kirk Cameron.

Maybe Mom understood what my secret world was all about. Either way, she did charge a price in exchange for turning a blind eye to my "secret" sojourns into her closet. From a young age I was tasked with helping keep the whole treasure trove organized and catalogued. A few random Saturdays a year, she would pull out a thick marker and some sticky labels and set them in front of me. I'd have to open each individual shoe box and write a description of the shoe on the sticky label before affixing it to the corresponding box. Then it was up to me to create an organizing system. Should the shoes be organized by box shape/size? By style? By color? Mom's only stipulation was that the sticker had to face outward so she could read the label at a quick glance.

I then did a similar thing with her leather coats and jackets, swapping out the coats according to season. And then I'd catalogue jewelry. This was our bonding activity. Mom would tell me stories

about where she got some of my favorite pieces. I heard tales of
what it was like being irreverently young and black down in Klan
country, where her college, Indiana University, was located. Tales
of black, sweaty bodies doing dances like the dawg and the hustle at
the annual Omega Psi Phi Mardi Gras party. Tales of the men my
mom loved long before she and my father became a thing. I stowed
away Mom's stories in the recesses of my soul, holding on to them
so I could share them with my future daughter. In that way, all of
her garments were as much mine as they were hers. Her taste was
my taste. Her past was my future.

And one day, just as I was nearing twelve, Mom took me back to
that Wilsons Leather store and let me pick out a leather jacket of
my own. She gave me the money to put down as a deposit, and it
would be my responsibility to use my allowance to pay down the
balance. Each time I got "paid," I would make my way to the mall
to put down that next installment, and I'd have to be diligent in my
payments so that my layaway wouldn't be closed due to inactivity.

I breezed into the Wilsons store this time, the smell of unworn
leather now an intoxicant. Leather made me feel tougher and fancier and special and chosen. And this jacket was going to be "the
one." It needed to reflect my own personal style, which was some
mash-up between girly and tomboy. I slowly worked my way through
the racks, searching for the one. At this age, I was growing into my
own, and one of the dope things about my mom was that (with the
rare exception when she'd declare something too grown for me) she
generally let my fashion and hair choices be what I wanted. She never
admonished me—neither did my dad—that a girl should act, talk,

sit, or dress like one thing in particular. I got to grow up feeling just as comfortable in dresses as I did in tennis shoes and my boy cousins' hand-me-downs.

The tomboy femme look would become a thing in the next few years because of singers like TLC and Aaliyah, who popularized baggy clothes on girls. I was ahead of the trend on this one: I was already into wearing "boy" clothes. Mom's own style and personality were definitely androgynous, so this wasn't odd to me. But I was nearing puberty, and it was becoming clear that outside of my household, little girls who "acted the part" were labeled well-behaved, and girls like me who were brash and loud and tomboyish were seen as a problem.

Still, that day I was drawn to the men's side of Wilsons. I was loving the boxier silhouettes of the men's jackets. I browsed, rack by rack, feeling and inhaling the rainbow of leather dreams. Finally, I found the one: it had a navy leather body with orange leather sleeves and a white leather hood. The lining was navy and white stripes. A zipper went down the front and the bottom was wide. It was super sporty, modeled after a windbreaker jacket. Mom's generation had made colored leather a thing in the early 80s. By the late 80s and early 90s, my hip hop generation was making multicolored leather a thing.

Mom thought the color clashing was a bit gaudy, kind of like how her father had felt that wearing a leather jacket was ostentatious in the 70s. But that wasn't the most important thing to her. My mother, with her closet full of red and teal leather, wanted her child to have exactly what she had: the confidence to know that what you wore was a statement of your personality, your beliefs, your politics. Mom's taste might be excessive, but I never thought she was materialistic, because everything she did just seemed so purposeful.

I walked over to the three-way mirror and tried my jacket on. It was a men's small. The orange sleeves hit at the middle of my palms. Too long, in Mom's mind, and the jacket *was* super wide on my frame. But to me the fit was perfect. My heart was set on it. And even though it wasn't her thing, Mom supported my choice. We walked over to the register together so I could put my first leather jacket on layaway.

3

Jheri Curl

For the record, *I never had a Jheri curl*. I had a Wave Nouveau. It's a subtle difference, but it matters. Okay, it doesn't matter to anyone outside of the cosmetology industry . . . which explains why I never did convince my classmates of the difference. They roasted a Wave Nouveau the same way they did a Jheri curl, that's for damn sure. But it mattered to me.

Hands down, the Jheri curl is the most maligned hairstyle in black history. It was the messiest, drip-droppiest, smelliest hair-style ever invented, it was a hazard to your furniture, and it was terrible for the health of your hair. The Wave Nouveau was supposed to be a dry curly perm that liberated Jheri curl victims from the dreaded plastic cap and couch-destroying activator sprays. The Wave Nouveau was the Jheri curl's classy, cosmopolitan cousin. Well, so I thought at age nine.

We look back at the 80s cold wave or curly perm era with chagrin and ask: Why the hell did we wear our hair like that? Why didn't we love ourselves more? We're ashamed that just on the other side of the Black Is Beautiful movement millions of us black folk traded our Afros for slick curls. But I am not ashamed of the fact that I rocked a style in the Jheri curl family. We front now, but the wash-and-go look that the cold wave afforded was the epitome of black LA glam back then. And low-key black folks are still getting cold waves to this day (do a YouTube search!). The Jheri curl was as big and bold and exuberant as the colorful makeup and chunky neon accessories that were on trend in the 80s. *Excess* was the name of the game. And this Midwestern girl wanted every bit of it.

I wanted a Wave Nouveau because my aunt Brenda had one. She and her husband had moved their family out to Los Angeles by then, leaving their middle-class, oak tree world of Fort Wayne to throw their classy soirees under the palm trees. I got to go out and visit for the summer when I was nine, just a month away from my tenth birthday. When we touched down in the city of stars, the plane could barely contain me. I bounded from my American Airlines seat and speed-walked down the corridor, my unaccompanied minor stewardess chasing after me. I scanned the crowd to find Aunt Brenda. "Teeny!" I heard her calling out the nickname she'd given me when I was a baby. There she was. Still the tall, slender goddess with skin the color of Cocoa Pebbles that I remembered. I wrapped my lanky arms around her neck and gave her a tight squeeze.

She was the same, but her hair was different, kind of like her surroundings, on a whole new level. In Fort Wayne, she had been sporting a bushy Afro-type hairstyle. But now, Aunt Brenda's tendrils were wavy and loose curls. Suddenly she had good hurrre! The kind of hair that moved when you tossed your head like the women in the Pantene commercials, the kind of hair that says "I got Indian in my family." It was cut in long layers, which hung just at her clavicle in a sleek style that she called a "bob." Before I could stop myself, I awkwardly raked my hands through the length of her hair, feeling the moist goodness of her just-out-of-the-shower curls.

I wanted *that* hair. My own hair was a dry sandy-brown color, coarse and tightly coiled. Good hair was aspirational hair for black girls like me, whose tender ears had been burned enough times by the hot comb to know that our kinks were damn near a threat to society. We had to keep them tamed by any means necessary.

By elementary school, I was already a beauty shop veteran, having bounced my narrow behind in and out of several local stylists' seats. My hair management had always been a thing, and I grew up understanding that I had obstinate, unruly hair. I typically had it in cornrows with beads, a style that Mom—who didn't know the first thing about doing black girl hair—could kinda handle. My hair frustrated my mother, who came from a family with "good," obedient hair with a looser curl pattern, which grew long and thick. Even though Mom mostly wore her hair closely shorn, she still knew on which bench she sat in the good hair game. She often reminded me that I had, unfortunately, inherited my resistant hair from my father's side of the family; it was as dusty as the red clay of the Alabama roads on which my grandparents had migrated north. On occasion, she took me to Mama Cokie's salon to have it pressed and curled, which made it easier to comb through but still required Mom to fix it up into neatly parted ponytails with knockers (the name we gave to the hair ties with colorful balls at the ends) and decorative barrettes. Now that Mom was a single parent with a demanding career, finding low-maintenance styling options had become a major issue. If only I didn't have these subversive kinks, I would be a good daughter for my overworked mom.

Many folks within and beyond the black community misguidedly think that black women's and girls' pursuit of good hair is somehow linked to a desire for whiteness. But really it isn't at all. Ask a black person what we mean when we say "good hair," and I bet not one will point to a white woman. I never wanted to have hair like the white girls at school with those stringy locks that smelled like wheat toast. I never once said I wanted to be white, though I did recognize that there was social currency in being a white girl in a town like mine. I also noticed that in my segregated community there was a premium placed on being a light-skinned black girl, though it would be years before I learned the rather academic term *colorism* (I think my first real introduction to the concept of a color hierarchy was through Spike Lee's *School Daze*). And for that reason, I had definitely asked God a time or two during my evening prayers to make me a few hues lighter. But for me, it wasn't even really about complexion. It was mostly about hair that was *easy*. No matter what shade you were, if you had that wash-and-go look, you were winning.

Most of the mainstream hair care commercials, which catered to white women, emphasized ease and convenience. Just fifteen minutes and you're ready to step out with confidence, they promised.

Fifteen minutes, that's where the allure was, instead of the hours I had to spend with my head and shoulders between some relative's knees getting my hair braided, or hours at Mama Cokie's salon smelling my burnt hair as she raked the hot comb from my roots to my ends. But I didn't want to have to be white to be carefree. I wanted to have long, loosely curled hair like my mom's sister Marcia and her daughter, Cheri, black women whose beauty rivaled that of any woman on television.

So when I saw Aunt Brenda's LA hair transformation, I wanted it so badly that I could've scalped her and worn her hair like a second skin. We pulled up to Aunt Brenda's new house in the Baldwin Hills neighborhood. Baldwin Hills was one of the wealthiest black enclaves in all of the United States, known colloquially as the black Beverly Hills. I craned my neck up to take in the expansiveness of their new house, which looked like a mansion to me. "Wait till you see the pool," Aunt Brenda's son, Tyrese, said to me. They had a pool in their backyard! Aunt Brenda had traded the cold Midwestern winters and urine-filled public pools for the high life in sunny LA, replete with a private pool and a cleaning lady. I, too, wanted to escape the shackles of my small factory town to live like my aunt Brenda. And in my newly concocted plan, I'd have the hair to match.

I spent my days splashing in the pool while Jermaine Stewart's "We Don't Have to Take Our Clothes Off" and Stacy Q's "Two of Hearts" thumped on the nearby boom box. When I was a baby, I had learned to swim at the Werling Street YMCA right across the street from Aunt Brenda's house. My family didn't have a membership, so she'd let my mother use her card to take me to the mommy-and-me infant swimming classes. I was even featured in the local newspaper. So, it was only fitting that, at nine-going-on-ten (going on twenty-one, in my mind), I was attempting wobbly dives into the deep aqua-blue waters of Aunt Brenda's luxury pool.

I felt shy about asking Aunt Brenda how she got her hair like that. I'd always been a precocious child who had to be reminded often by the adults to "stay outta grown folks' business" when I interjected into their gossipy conversations. But black girls learn early that a sista's hair is a sensitive subject, a secret between her and her hairstylist. After seeing Aunt Brenda surface from the pool with glamorous waves just as intact as they were before her dip, while my hair became a tight Afro in the water, I worked up the courage to ask. "It's a Wave Nouveau," she told me. A Wave Nouveau. It even sounded glamorous! I knew the word *nouveau* meant "modern" or "current" in French because I had looked it up in the dictionary after the R&B group Club Nouveau started releasing a string of hits like "Why You Treat Me So Bad" and "Lean on Me." Wave Nouveau. Modern wave. In hip hop parlance, it meant a "fresh 'do."

I had so many questions, and my doting aunt answered each one. She told me—with the enthusiasm of someone on the SoftSheen-Carson (the company that made Wave Nouveau) marketing team—that the Wave Nouveau was a new permanent curl system that loosened the curl pattern, giving the wearer a full head of body waves. The products didn't make your hair wet and greasy like a Jheri curl. Instead they left your hair with a patina that screamed healthy. Aunt Brenda pulled her products down from a high shelf in her marbled bathroom. "See," she said, "they smell good too." I inhaled a nostril full of the curl mist, which came in a teal cylindrical bottle with WAVE NOUVEAU written in metallic purple letters. I asked Aunt Brenda if I could spray a bit of the magic elixir on my hair. She obliged. And I released a thin mist of berry-scented chemicals that saturated my kinky edges. I savored the moment, rubbing in the jelly-like activator as if the spray itself could convert my tight kinks into Aunt Brenda's body waves.

Every year as I inched closer to puberty, it became clearer to me that there was this complex sorcery crucial to black womanhood, and I was gonna have to become an alchemist. The magic in these Wave Nouveau bottles was all part of the smoke and mirrors game. You see, it was fine for a black man to wear a Jheri curl and everyone know that's not his real hair texture. But a black woman had to be a bit slicker about it. She needed to present an entire package that would suggest that she was the type of woman who *could* have been born with good hair. My aunt Brenda looked the part: she had a cold wave that was more wave than curl, just the right texture.

All of this was of course bound up in class politics. Aunt Brenda lived in an exclusive milieu, and she drove a shiny black Mercedes-Benz. While a drippy Jheri curl might have passed in Fort Wayne, it most certainly would not have in Los Angeles. By this time, the Jheri curl, which had been cool when it debuted, was definitely seen as a working-class 'do. No respectable upper-class black woman or rising starlet would be caught dead in a Jheri curl, whose smell of hot plastic and ammonia, tempered by hints of Queen Helene Cocoa Butter, announced its presence a mile away, especially on a hot day. Women like Aunt Brenda, who were vying for spots in the closed ranks of the black LA elite, needed to be *unclockable*. No one better be able to detect by sight or smell that her curls were chemically enhanced. And that was the magic promised by Wave Nouveau products.

These products were the most expensive ones on the market at that time—SoftSheen-Carson was making its customers pay a premium to not smell like battery acid. And the tacky plastic bag used to keep the Jheri curl moist also separated the haves from the have-nots. In fact, commercials for the Leisure Curl, which, like the Wave Nouveau, was a dry perm marketed toward black professional women, used the tagline "zap that cap!" The camera pans toward a black woman in a stylish black suit with her hair in a chic French twist, presumably on her way to work. The point is that you can't even tell that she is wearing a cold wave. Her hair blends into her business surroundings, allowing her to blend in equally smoothly in the corporate world. She's not a woman with a collar stained by Jheri curl "juice." In the movies, folks working in fast food and other low-wage jobs were wearing plastic bag curls. The class lines had been drawn in the pop culture sand. And I knew which life I wanted.

Little did I know, the luxe Wave Nouveau had a humble origin story much like my own. It started with Robert "Jheri" Redding. Redding is known for being the godfather of the modern curly perm . . . for white people. Like me, Redding grew up in a small Midwestern town and had dreams of living the big-city life in LA. After building his popularity as a hairstylist in Chicago, he relocated to Los Angeles in the 1940s and used chemistry and smart branding to build an empire of successful hair-care brands like Redken and Nexxus. By the 70s, he was on top of his game, and his curly perms were rising in popularity, but they were still just designed for and marketed to white people.

Enter Dr. Willie Morrow. He was the man who had commercialized the Afro picks that kept my dashiki parents' halo 'fros in perfect shape in the 70s. Now he hustled the permanent wave processes that Redding had developed for straight hair and perfected them for black folks like me whose natural hair texture was tightly coiled, aka nappy. In order to make a curly perm work for black folks, Morrow had figured out, you had to create a two-step process. And the key to the entire process was what he called curl "activator," a liquid that you kept reapplying to your curls to give them life. Activator. It sounded real futuristic, and it came along at just the right time for the market.

You see, Los Angeles had a long history of being the epicenter of black hair-care innovation, because it was the heart of the film and music industries, and the politics of visibility drove a lot of that. When the halo Afro was the look du jour, black hairstylists and chemists focused on techniques and products to make Afros maximally huge and tightly curled, creating the image of the hip, conscious soul sista and soul brotha. If your hair didn't kink up just right, it couldn't hold that big halo Afro look. So by the mid-1970s, there started to be an uprising from the light-skinned, biracial, and otherwise kinky-challenged black women who felt as if the Black Is Beautiful movement had created a reverse hierarchy and now their loose, curly hair was considered unattractive and not authentically black.

Light-skinned women fought back with their pocketbooks, demanding products and advertisements that reflected *their* natural beauty. And hair-care lines from Afro Sheen to Raveen Au Naturelle started responding: now it was the "new natural" that was in. And just like that, kinky-haired black women who had found themselves atop the black beauty totem pole during the Black Power era were once again struggling to make their hair do this latest look.

I'd watch the glamour goddesses in TV ads in the early 80s when the trend was still going strong—they were all Jayne Kennedy look-alikes. Kennedy was tall and fair skinned with features that looked like she indeed had *Indian* in her family. Her long, massively thick, curly tresses cascaded down her back, stopping just before the curve of her tiny hourglass frame. That was the *aspirational* hair. And for some reason, everyone wanted that curly look cut into a mullet shape: short on the top and sides, long in the back.

So Morrow had captured lightning in a bottle for the good-hair challenged. He had been developing his cold wave technique since 1971, but now the social and political stage was set for a change, and he was ready to capitalize. Morrow branded his product the California Curl and began selling the line and teaching the method to black stylists in LA in the late 1970s. From the Jackson 5 to New Edition to model-actress Ola Ray to gangsta rap group N.W.A., black celebs and beauty and fashion influencers were rocking the excessively wet curls. Even a young Whitney Houston wore a closely cropped cold wave in the early 1980s. Images of her in curls ran on the cover of *Seventeen* magazine and in Max Factor ads before record exec Clive Davis rebranded her image and plopped Whitney into bouffant wash-and-go wigs.

Jheri Redding was no dummy. He knew that Morrow's cold wave system could offer him the entrée he needed to expand his empire into the still-segregated black hair-care market. All he had to do was buy a patent for Morrow's two-step process. Morrow was more of a chemist and teacher than a shrewd businessman. He gave everyone, including Redding, access to his multibillion-dollar-grossing formula, and watched all those dollars flow away from his California Curl brand to line other pockets. Redding, on the other hand, was a marketing Svengali, and he made Morrow's process synonymous with *his* brand: the Jheri curl. He launched Jheri curl in 1978, and he won the name game hands down: even though every

hair-care company, black and white, ended up with their own version of the product by the mid-80s, the style will forever be known
as the Jheri curl. Just like that, Redding had positioned himself as
the patron saint of nappy-haired black folks across the country.

So the Jheri curl was in, and every company was selling it. And
for the style to work, you had to use activator. Letting a curl dry
out exposed how much the harsh chemicals had damaged the hair,
made it look more like the now passé Afro. Black men and women
alike were spending upward of $500 a year to keep their curls coated
in aqueous chemicals, dripping all over shirt collars, pillowcases,
and loveseats in the struggle. Plastic bags even became something
of a hair accessory in the hood that could unabashedly be worn
outdoors—kind of like paper hair setting tape and silver marcel
wave clips had been in the jazz age. You saw someone in a bag, you
understood they were just protecting their hair investment.

But all those ruined couches got old. By the time I wanted my
own cold wave, making fun of the activator "technology" was a staple
of comedy. Who could forget Robert Townsend's 1987 satire *Hollywood Shuffle*, in which the criminal is actually named, of all things,
Jheri Curl?! The product itself even plays a big role in the film. The
evil Jheri Curl is swinging his wild locks and dramatically dousing
them in activator, spraying the stuff all over the gym, when the hero,
Ace, comes in. At one point, Ace manages to grab that curl juice and
threatens to spill it. Curl is clearly addicted to his activator. As the
plot ricochets forward, we see his locks get drier and drier and poofier and poofier, his greasy villain look reverting to a tightly coiled
Afro without the aid of the all-important curl activator.

Then there's Eddie Murphy's 1988 classic *Coming to America*. The
film's villain, Darryl, is heir to a Jheri curl empire called Soul

Glo. He and his entire family leave curl juice stains on furniture everywhere they go. Man, did we die laughing at those curl juice scenes. I remember hearing some pretty crude jokes about women with Jheri curls too: "No one wants to be with a woman who smells like a chemistry set!" and "That ain't the kind of juice you want drenching your sheets when you take a woman to bed."

But the image burned into my young mind is Michael Jackson dancing down the stairs, doing his signature pelvic thrusts and finger points, as his hair goes up in *flames*. Everybody has to have witnessed the King of Pop's near-death experience because the tragedy was caught on tape and broadcast on loop across our television screens. This was 1984. Jackson was taping a Pepsi commercial in front of a live audience, a lucky crowd getting to see all his dance moves up close and personal. Of course, he had to have some pyrotechnics in his show. Suddenly, one of the sparks must have set his chemical-doused Jheri curl on fire—but he didn't realize it! Michael whipped into a series of lightning-speed turns at the foot of the stairs as the blaze on top of his head burned bright yellow and orange. Crew members tackled him with blankets to smother the fire as we all gasped.

The Jheri curl was downright dangerous. Jackson suffered third-degree burns and continued to have migraine headaches for years after the incident. Still, Michael didn't stop wearing the hairstyle. And neither did we. The curl stayed in high demand among the everyday black folks in the farmlands and Rust Belt cities in Middle America. When I saw my aunt Brenda's Wave Nouveau, I knew that she was onto something that Fort Wayne folks did not have access to.

But what I didn't know was that my obsession with my aunt Brenda's cold wave would put me in the center of a politically and socially charged Jheri curl marketing war. I just wanted some way to bottle up the carefree black girlness that I had experienced in Los Angeles. At home, I'd kind of shrunk away into my own tiny, tight little exile from everything after my parents' divorce. Here in LA, I was open and unbounded as I took in my surroundings: the Hollywood Hills, Disneyland, Venice Beach. I wasn't a burden on anyone or a problem that needed to be solved. And people in LA were chill and relaxed, their luxury lifestyles were filled with leisurely activities, unlike my parents and my friends' parents, who were just always working, grinding.

I wanted this LA life, where instead of a cop Aunt Brenda was a foodie. She opened a catering company called Munchies, so she was making things now. But not like a button for a car part that some factory had demanded 10 thousand pieces of—she was making things out of her own ingenuity. I wanted her life. In my young mind, the luxury pool, the trendsetting fashion, the California sun, and that carefree hair all became synonymous. *All* of my little black girl desires could be realized if I could just get a Wave Nouveau.

When I returned to Fort Wayne, I went on and on to Mom about Aunt Brenda's hair and how I had to get mine done just like hers. It occurs to me now that here I was droning on about how I wanted to look like her best friend, not her. But whatever pangs of jealousy she might have felt, she never showed them.

Mom did a little research and learned that a local veteran stylist, Cheryl, was trained to apply the magic products. I was shocked. I didn't think anyone in Fort Wayne would have even been up on Wave Nouveau. What I didn't know was that the whole thing wasn't as big a revolution as I thought. SoftSheen-Carson had revamped the leaky activator sprays into dry mists, firm gels, and lotion-like emollients to dodge the Soul Glo image. But the dry curl really used the same two-step chemical process that Morrow had developed and Redding had copied and popularized. So anyone who had been taught to apply a Jheri curl could do one of its newer, hipper, bougie cousin styles like the Wave Nouveau.

Cheryl quoted the cost of the process at $65 and said it took three to four hours to complete. I saw Mom bracing herself at the price. But she made me an appointment. I mean, $65 for a ten-year-old's hair in 1989? That was an insane amount of money. But Mom couldn't do hair. Like, at all. And she was willing to pay for the convenience of not having to mess with it for months. With the press-and-curl I'd been wearing, she had to take me to Mama Cokie's shop every two weeks and then still had to mess with the ponytails and baubles. This new look was going to be carefree for me *and* for her. Win-win.

Mom dropped me off for my appointment and Cheryl walked me through the process. I could see the huge vats in Wave Nouveau's signature teal and purple from my chair. This was definitely the real thing!

I liked how Cheryl was explaining things to me as she would to one of her paying adult clients. I was taking my new commitment to managing my own hair very seriously. So, the first step was to apply a creamy formula that straightened the hair, cleverly called a "shape rearranger." That sounded so much cooler than the caustic relaxers that had been around for decades, although the shape rearranger's job was, in fact, to relax your kinks and make your hair nice and straight. Cheryl opened up the bottle, and the smell made my nostrils burn, nothing at all like Aunt Brenda's bottles. Here I was at ten, exposing my virgin scalp to a chemical cocktail strong enough to leave me bald—all in the name of beauty and desire and aspiration.

Cheryl carefully sectioned my hair, applying the thick cream from root to tip. I had to let it sit there so long, I made my way through two black hair magazines. The chemical was slowly heating up as I flipped the pages, the heat from my scalp serving as a catalyst. And *just* before the chemicals could burn my scalp, Cheryl rushed me to the shampoo bowl chair to get it all out. She rubbed and massaged my scalp, making the nape of my neck tingle. Her hands ran through my hair with no resistance. *This is what the girls with good hair must experience all the time*, I thought, that feeling of hands touching directly on your scalp with no nappy kinks to get in the way.

Cheryl draped a towel around my head before lifting me back up and walking me over to the styling chair. She combed my hair down flat with a thin-toothed comb. Never had anyone been able to comb through my hair with a thin white people's comb—this stuff truly was a miracle cream! My hair always needed something with wide teeth. I had learned this the hard way after trying to tease my hair like I'd seen Madonna do in her film *Desperately Seeking Susan*. I had found a fine-toothed comb and reached up, trying to imitate Madonna. The comb got stuck almost right away, and I couldn't get it out. I got impatient and yanked the thing and damn near yanked half my hair out. So I had to spend forever disengaging one strand at a time so I could loose the comb without losing whole chunks of my hair.

But now Cheryl was stroking through my hair like it was silk. When she turned me around to face the mirror, I saw my reddish-brown tresses hung well past my shoulders. My hazel eyes bugged out in disbelief. I could not believe that my hair was that long. The back was even longer than the sides, which touched the faded vinyl smock that Cheryl had draped over me. And Cheryl took a moment from her work to give me a smile that I registered in the mirror on the wall in front of us. Surely she had experienced this moment before, giving little black girls their first chemical treatment and seeing the look of awe in their eyes as they met their new (true?) selves. I ran my fingers through my hair and flung it back and forth the way I liked to make my friends LaKendra and LaShonda do at recess. That was their penance for having good, curly hair: they had to shake it for me like the white women in the Pantene commercials whenever I demanded. But now, I could shake my own bone-straight hair.

I could feel Cheryl drag the cold, dull end of her cutting shears against my neck as she spliced her way through my locks, sculpting them into my desired bob. She lifted my limp hair, expertly creating layers, cutting off what seemed like these precious inches I had only just met. No sooner discovered, then discarded, dropping to the floor beneath the hydraulic styling chair. Once the cutting stopped, my hair didn't look like much. It was definitely shorter than Aunt Brenda's. Sensing the look of disappointment that was beginning to creep up on the corners of my mouth, she said, "It'll look much fuller once the curl is set."

Okay, so this was the second step in the process. Now it was time for the "shape former," another cream that Cheryl smoothed into my new tresses. She began parting out thin slivers of hair with a rat-tailed comb. She lifted each section to the tips and then rolled a perm rod all the way down to my roots. I could see myself in the mirror, my head a crazy ball of large orange and smaller lavender rods sticking this way and that. One thing that made the Wave Nouveau appear different was using larger rods (13/16 and 11/16) to make a looser S-shape—the original Jheri curl usually used thin rods for tight curls. And the larger the wave the more your hair's length would show.

Back to the sink for a dousing in a thick liquid called a "neutralizer," which Cheryl carefully applied with a straight-tip applicator. The whole logic of the process was getting really wack at this point. So, the chemicals in the neutralizer do the exact opposite as those of the shape rearranger. The rearranger broke the protein bonds in the hair to straighten the kinks; then the neutralizer caused new protein bonds to form, this time in the shape of the rods that Cheryl had put in my hair.

The neutralizer was gonna give my hair its new life, but it smelled like death. It was the kind of thick sulfur smell that got into your mouth and clung to your taste buds as if you had snacked on it. I didn't think there could be anything that smelled worse; none of my conviction that this was the way to LA style could stop me from recoiling at this toxic waste being smeared on my head. Cheryl put a plastic bag over my hair and left this solution on for almost a full episode of *The People's Court* while she busied herself with relaxing and marcel curling her other clients.

Glamorous Aunt Brenda drifted into my mind. There she was, rising from the pool, with the mermaid allure of that good hair. To look at her nowadays, I bet no one in LA could tell she was from this dreary Fort Wayne—and in LA, standards were everything. She had attained the secrets of the sisterhood of fashionistas in the most vanity-driven city you'd ever find. And now *I* was getting the magic potion to wash away my factory-town residue. Rusty lil' Fort Wayne wouldn't even recognize me as its own.

Cheryl once again. She turned on the rubber spray hose, shooting water through every crevasse in the nest of rods to make sure there was no trace left of the toxic neutralizer. She took me to the hydraulic chair once again and pumped it three times, one, two, three, until my face bounced up into the mirror. She carefully unwound each rod, so as not to disturb the wet infant curl that it had helped to birth. Now I started to see it: my new bob that fell perfectly, thickly into a wavy wash-and-go look. She squeezed some of the lotion-y curl activator from a teal bottle into her hands, emulsifying it between her palms before smoothing it through my hair. There was that smell I remembered from Aunt Brenda's bottles, it brought a Baldwin Hills breeze right there into stifling Indiana. Now Cheryl was shaking and bopping my curls all over, releasing them to spring out and play around like black girls on hopscotch squares. She finished the look with some of the dry mist spray.

Cheryl next took a wide-tooth comb and feathered out the layers of my bob. Now I looked less like my aunt Brenda and more like Sweet L.D., a member of the rap duo Oaktown's 357, who wore her hair in a similar auburn-colored wavy bob. That was fine by me. Sweet L.D. was my girl! When I got home, I told myself, I would put a little gel on my front edges to make my bang wave and stand up, just like Sweet L.D.'s. Whether I was emulating my LA auntie or my rap idol from Oakland, I looked like a Cali girl.

Cheryl instructed me on how to care for my cold wave in between visits. I was to wash and condition it every two weeks. Each night, I should put a little of the creamy curl moisturizer in my hair. I didn't have to sleep with a plastic bag on it, but if I did, it would help retain some moisture. In the morning, I should rake more of the curl activator through my locks and style however I wanted. I could wear it up in a ponytail, or half up, half down, or all down to showcase the precise stacks (black girl language for layers) of my bob. That was it. My hair would retain the moist wash-and-go look every day without me actually having to wash it daily. And I didn't have to come back until my roots started to grow out and I could feel the coarse, kinky texture of my hair return. So basically, I'd need a touchup by the time I got my next report card.

This was, of course, long before the healthy hair turn in black hair styling in the early 2000s, when stylists started stressing the importance of coming for regular deep conditioning and trimming. Back in my cold wave days, stylists had really bought into the marketing dream that Redding and other hair-care conglomerates in the cold wave battle had sold them: that this hair was truly carefree. That somehow finding a way to chemically replicate "good" wash-and-go hair—which we *imagined* didn't have to be maintained—meant that you *actually* didn't have to maintain it, despite the fact that they had just applied several harsh, extremely drying chemicals to the hair and scalp and were now selling you a basket of additional accoutrements to maintain it with. My non-hairstyling mother and my ten-year-old self would now be charged with the diligent maintenance of this chemically treated mop of hair. It actually compared very poorly to a Chia Pet or a betta fish on the list of things you can care for in a carefree manner. But I was going to cherish and nurture my Wave Nouveau, so it was all good.

When I woke up the next day, it was as though I was waking up in a movie. My hair was thoroughly moist and wavy. I ran my fingers through it. There should have been some new jack swing song playing in the background, Teddy Riley offering a hype "Yep, yep!" of approval. I had done such a good job following Cheryl's directions: it was not dry. It was perfect. I could definitely wear it down today and show off my dope stacks. So I slathered on an extra coating of activator and began my short trek to Village Elementary school where my Wave Nouveau and I could make our debut.

Still in the early weeks of the fall semester, it was sunny with a touch of humidity lingering in the air. Over the weeks, the late-September sun would interact with the cold wave chemicals, turning my already sandy locks an even bolder honey blond at the tips. But for now, I marched along from the tic-tac-size low-income apartment we'd moved to after my parents' divorce through the winding house-lined streets that made up the outer fringes of the Village Woods neighborhood.

My hair would do my boasting today, tacitly reminding my classmates of their own cultural inadequacies. They didn't have the access I did to all things fashion-forward and West Coast. When the first boy in my grade saw me, his eyes beamed. I paused and waited, ready to receive his compliment like a fourth-grade queen.

"Ahhhhh, Tanisha got a Jheri curl!" rang out through the entire vestibule. This was not the response I was expecting. I launched into my explanation: "This is a Wave Nouveau," I said in a sassy voice tinted with a bit of nerdiness, hand on my bony hip, neck rollin', "something completely diff . . ." But before I could even finish, more boys started to crowd around me, taunting me about my hair. "Follow the drip, follow the drip!" one said, mimicking comedian Robin

Harris. "Where's your plastic cap?" "Nitroglycerin!" Others just followed behind me making guttural sounds like Michael Jackson: "Ah! Ch'umon." When you grow up in a majority black neighborhood and are raised in predominantly black schools, you're used to being cracked on or roasted, and you learn to give as good as you get. It wasn't personal. It was just the culture. So, not what I expected, but okay. I stood up straight and faced my verbal assailants with a few of my own witty retorts: "Shut up Eric, witcho crusty nose! Yo boogers got boogers!" And, "Pooh, why yo pants always look like you got 'em from yo three-year-old brother?? You stay floodin' like a mug!"

So this back-and-forth between me and a dozen loudmouthed boys ran on all morning, like an unoriginal HBO comedy special on Jheri curls, interrupted by classes. We kept firing off shots during phys ed and art and into lunch.

But by the time we hit afternoon recess, my hair had grown weary of the battle. My activator had quit on me. My wet and wavy look was now parched and poofy. And here was the real horror of the thing: *I had no activator with me.* I was a recent convert, so I never even thought to bring curl activator in my book bag (which, truth be told, probably would've gotten me roasted even more. I'm talkin' *excoriated*!). And it got even worse, as I dug around in my bag, I didn't even have a hair tie to pull my locks up into a messy ponytail with.

And then: "Ooooh, you curl is drrrrryyyyyy!" (in a voice like a whisper, as if to simulate a parched throat). That was it, they had me. I was surrounded by black boys from all four of the fourth-grade classes, in an uproar of laughter. "Jheri curl, Jheri curl! But where's the juice?" At first, I tried to stand my ground, managing to eke out a "shut up" as I chased one of the boys who was shorter than me around. I had fistfought several of these boys at some earlier point in time. But they were too much for me today. I felt tears welling up. I couldn't let these boys see me cry. I sought refuge with some of my girlfriends.

By now, I could feel my hair was standing all over my head in a soft, limp Afro. I didn't have enough juice to keep a curl, and I didn't have enough kink left after the hair-straightening agents to have a Black Power halo Afro. I asked my friend Ayesha how bad it looked. She didn't want to tell me the truth. But as a good friend, she diplomatically suggested that I go the ponytail route. So we began traveling along the black girl underground railroad, querying all of the black girls that we had a friend connection with to see if they had a spare knocker or hair clip. No luck.

Michelle, a girl in my grade who had a Leisure Curl, schooled me, in all of her cold curl wisdom, about why she never wore her hair down on the first day she got her curl touched up. Yeah, yeah. I didn't have time for her sanctimony. I was in a black girl *crisis* here.

The classroom was no escape. The boys continued to walk by, dropping off taunts as they crossed by my desk. Some even passed notes with illustrations of what a curl should look like versus my dry mop top. The humiliation finally caught up to me, and, panicking, I asked my teacher, Mr. Green, for a bathroom pass. I locked myself in the single-stall bathroom and gave in to the tears that had been wanting to fall since recess. I looked at myself in the mirror, spirit wounded, and perceived the tousled, nameless, shapeless, in-between mess that all my elegant plans had morphed into.

With the last few ounces of dignity left in me, I devised a plan: What if I repurposed the neon pink lanyard cord that I kept secured around my faux tortoise-shell glasses and used it as a hair tie?

Sniffle.

That cord, which I had picked out so confidently earlier that year when my eye doctor told me I was nearsighted and would need glasses, would be my lifeline.

Breathe.

I carefully removed the clear rubber loops from my big framed glasses and started trying to find the best way to make this all work, without the aid of a brush or comb or anything at all with elastic properties. I tried to gather my hair up into a high ponytail. No luck. With my new bob cut, the back layers were too short. I started again, this time gathering the ponytail as low as possible, and managed to get it all in my hand that way. I started wrapping the pink cord tight. I needed some way to secure the loop. Nothing came to me. I couldn't solve this problem, and the whole thing fell apart. I broke down, in total defeat, crying the type of ugly cry that you have after big mama tells you to go break a *switch* off a tree in the backyard. That was it. I was defeated. I was broken.

I wasn't thin-skinned by any means. I was used to them singing "Have you driven a Ford lately?," like the people in the popular car commercial. I wasn't really bothered when they called me "Jolly Green Giant" when I walked by, on account that I had experienced a growth spurt and was already 5'1" at ten years old and towered over everyone in class. I could even handle them calling me "sperm teller" and "sperm technologist" after I explained during science class (my favorite subject at the time) that male frogs release sperm in order to fertilize an egg. I had glasses and wore a clunky mouthpiece called a "Bionator" that made me speak with a lisp. The boys would call out, "Hi Thaneeesstha," imitating my thick, tongue-heavy pronunciations. I got it. I was a nerd. I wasn't ashamed of that. I had always had witty comebacks for those jokes because I was proud to be a nerd, thought glasses were actually a cool accessory, and knew that one day I would no longer have a gap and an overbite.

But this hit the way a really good crack does. Those cracks sucker punch you where you're really vulnerable, showing you parts of yourself that you may not have wanted to see and for damn sure don't want anyone else to see.

And it wasn't necessarily about my hair. I mean, yes, my hair was the battleground on this particular day. But this was about the whole dream life I'd smoothed into my bouncy curls evaporating into pure fantasy. They clowned me for having a Jheri curl, and my insistence that what I had was everything but that—that it was California and private pools and sophisticated friends in the know on every trend—was absolutely meaningless to them and just egged them on. To them, a Leisure Curl was a Care Free Curl was a Wave Nouveau.

I'd been living in an inner fantasy world since my parents' divorce. LA had made me feel safe enough to dream out loud. Now these boys had stomped my little black girl dreams. Socked my haughtiness like a half-inflated tetherball. Who was I to think that I was any better than anyone else here? Who was I to think that I could get out, that a hairstyle would make me special?

I kept my curl for the remainder of the school year, occasionally plopping down in Cheryl's sturdy chair for a touch-up. But with every day that passed between me and my California summer, I found myself slowly sinking back under the mandates of the factory town. I tucked my dreams away again. When I entered fifth grade, I had a regular relaxer like all of the other girls.

Tennis Shoes

I learned at a very young age that wearing the wrong color shoes can get you bashed in the head with a roller skate. This was a lesson taught at the expense of Mike Read, the redbone boy all the girls loved because he had that *good* hair that made the ends of his cornrows curl up just right. Mike ran with a gang that hung out at Roller Dome South, but everybody knew he was from a good family and really wasn't about that thug life. People just let him front like he was. Until that bloody night. I strolled in with my crew of friends in my grade for the monthly all-night skate party.

All us black teens and preteens made this rink our haven. The referees looked like us, the music was hip hop and R&B. You had to come correct at the Roller Dome. How you looked and who you hung with determined if you left getting the nod from the cool older folks or slumped over in the backseat crying.

Cincinnati Reds and Georgetown Hoyas jackets flooded the rink that night. The CPTs (Claiming Pontiac [Street] Territory or ComPTon, depending on who you ask), a People-affiliated gang known for wearing red, sported the big white Cincinnati C emblazoned on red jackets. The BGDs (Black Gangster Disciples), part of the Folk gang family that wore dark blue, rocked the royal blue G of the Hoyas. And both gangs looked extra fly because they had color-coordinated Nike Dopemans (aka Cortez) too, the shoe that dominated our fashion scene in those days.

Like most black kids I knew, I had grown up at the skating rink. My parents threw my third birthday party there, slicing neat pieces of chocolate Miss Piggy birthday cake, skating to the "Hokey Pokey" at the center of the rink. I traded in the busted "brownies," the name we gave to the dookie-colored rental skates, for my sharp pink speed skates around the time that I became old enough to attend all-night skate parties. I was never really that skilled at skating, unlike my mom, who grooved on her white speed skates on weekends when she wasn't working. I was strictly there for the socializing! All-night skating was basically a church group lock-in, without the religious talk and prayer, and instead with plenty of grinding and very few chaperones. Our parents would drop us off before eleven p.m. and the party would pulse all night until six a.m., the referees—only slightly older than us—becoming our cheap, and sometimes negligent, babysitters. Everyone else's parents, that is.

As in everywhere else in my life, it seemed, my mother's constant presence was cramping my style, because she worked security at the monthly all-night skate parties to earn extra income.

We made our way inside, and I scanned the room to see who was already here. The thump of the 808s as "Drop the Bass" by DJ Magic Mike—the man who breathed new life into Miami bass music—banged through the speakers and put a little bounce in our steps. I looked to see if fine-ass Larry, my favorite referee, was there. He was whizzing around on his black speed skates like a ghetto Wayne Gretzky. (Years later, my older cousin married Larry. I was so jealous!) We strolled over to the concession stand to fill up on sour pickles, Now and Laters, and cheese sludge–covered nachos.

And then screaming. Screaming and yelling loud enough to drown out MC Breed's "Ain't No Future in Yo Frontin'" on the sound system. A mob of black teens poured over to the east side of the rink, slamming up against the baby blue quarter lockers. Another gang fight. I never understood why people run *to* the fight. Despite having my own rep as a lil' brawler, my inner voice always said to flee. But a desire to stick with my friends overrode my natural instincts. I dashed from the concessions counter and then slithered around the outer edges of the crowd where my friends had gathered to get a look. Mom stopped mid-stride in front of me and yelled, "Get yo ass back to the counter!" It was like she had LoJack on my skates; she always knew where I was in that massive rink. This was becoming part of our routine. Mom worked security at every teen party around the city. And at every party a fight would break out and she'd find me and yell at me to "get back!" or "go home!" before the officers released pepper spray when they couldn't physically break up the fight. This night, I saw her dart into the center of the crowd, instructing folks to "move back!" The fight was over almost as soon as it started. No pepper spray tonight.

The gossip was filtering through the crowd now: the CPTs had jumped Mike Read, pounded him with the business end of their expensive speed skates. Some say they saw his face as my mom and the other cops pulled him out of the melee; he was almost unrecognizable. His eyes were swollen shut, lips busted, and the whole left side of his face sagged unnaturally. Blood covered his beautiful braids. The CPTs had beaten Mike Read to the white meat. Mike Read, the pretty boy who was loyal to royal blue Dopemans, got caught for a split second without his BGD buddies, and CPTs with a score to settle surrounded him in a sea of red and gave him that work. I was too far back to view the action, but by the time I started middle school, I'd seen this same thing go down plenty of times. And when I think of being a black girl on the cusp of teendom, the gang violence, the thrills of the skating rink, the rise of sneaker culture, and the nadir of the crack epidemic meld into one giant memory. Mike Read's beating is shorthand for all of it.

The gang culture of the late 1980s and early 90s had a huge impact on the fashion in my factory town, and on the rest of the country. The late 1980s were perilous times for us. We were trying the best we could to survive as the Reagan era folded into the Bush I years. Deindustrialization hit Fort Wayne hard, and as economic instability shook apart our old social order, the once minor underground economy bloomed into a full-fledged ecosystem. Instability breeds decay, and crack cocaine took root in that decay like fungus. Times got bleaker. Money got tighter. But hip hop fashion was starting to become a thing, and it gave us a sense of power.

Fashion trends were still regional in the late 1980s. But hip hop culture was going national. The most powerful boys at the rink would wear dark-wash Levi's or Dickies jeans or Dickies 874 Originals in khaki or black. Either way, they were always freshly pressed with a precision that would make the folks at Niagara Spray Starch proud. They wore flannels, tall tees, or hoodies in their gang colors, often layered over a crisp white t-shirt or ribbed tank, which folks crassly called "wife beaters" or "O-Dogs," after the *Menace II Society* character. Those garments had been part of our parents' factory uniforms for decades. They made sense to us long before some rapper who lived thousands of miles away told us they were cool to wear.

Local stores—from Value City to JCPenney—sold those Dickies work khakis and flannels and hoodies in bulk. But then those distant rappers popped up on BET and MTV right in our living rooms, and our look suddenly had national cachet. Gang members had their own fashion rules, but the rest of us had our hip hop looks drawn from the same hood stylebook. And all of a sudden we were making demands of our parents' checkbooks in ways we hadn't when we were in elementary school and pretty much wore whatever they bought. We were teenagers now. We had to look the part. We had to be people who could be recognized as somebody. Hip hop culture was where it was at, coast to coast and in the middle states too. We were hip hop. We wanted the athletic team apparel and the crisp midnight-wash jeans and the tennis shoes. We *had* to have the tennis shoes. I never questioned why we called those soft-soled athletic status symbols tennis shoes when absolutely nobody played tennis. It's just how the Midwest says it.

Back then, everybody wanted a pair of Nike Cortez, which we called "Dopemans." You have to be from a certain part of the country to even know what I'm talking about when I say Dopemans.

When I started looking into the history of the shoe, I called up old friends from home to ask if they remembered when the Nike Cortez was the shit. "What's a Cortez?" they'd say. But if I said, "You know, Dopemans," they'd light up. Seemed like everyone had a pair. Across the country, kids had different names for the shoe. In LA, Latinos called them "Air Cholos" or "Los Nikes de Cholo." In Oklahoma, they were called "Milkshakes." No one seems to know why, but it might be because cocaine was called ice cream and the coke dealer the ice-cream man. The Texas and Louisiana region called them "Gangsta Nikes," "G-Nikes," or "Project Nikes" (Nikes being one syllable instead of ni-ke like most folks say it). Like us, Atlanta and the upper South called the Cortez "Dopemans," as did parts of the Midwest north of Indiana. Other variants included "Bullet Nikes" or "Two Strikes," 'cuz people who wore them were one strike away from getting a life sentence in prison. All across the country folks like me associated this shoe with gang life, with street life and hip hop. We were reverencing the same ghetto superstars as kids in other parts of the country, even when we used different words.

By any name, athletic shoes were essential gear for a lot of kids in the late 80s and early 90s. Jordans have cast a long shadow in the history of hip hop sneaker culture. But no one in Fort Wayne was really wearing Js in my middle school days. We were a frugal town; those shoes were far too expensive, even for those of us kids whose anxiously-barely-middle-class parents were constantly soothing their economic angst by buying us things. Jordans were a little too flamboyant even for us. Fort Wayne kids were mostly rockin' Dopemans, Reebok Classics and 5411s, shell toes and Gazelles by Adidas, K-Swiss Classic 88s, and Diadora B. Elites. If you were really fancy, you had a pair of British Knights, Troops, Filas, or maybe

Nike Air Force 1s. I did own a pair of quilted pink-on-white British Knights, or "BKs," as we called them. I begged my mom for those shoes and then got bored of them before I could even break them in good. Mom swore she wouldn't buy me another pair of tennis shoes. (She was trippin'. She loved buying me the latest styles just as much as I loved having them.) So I wasn't that turned on by the tennis shoe culture, personally. But I watched what the lust for the latest shoes seemed to be doing to my neighborhood. They created a desire so intense that my friends were willing to cross over into the dark side of drugs and gangs to get them.

And drugs and gangs were all around us in those days. The crack cocaine trade spread from South America to ports in Los Angeles and Miami. From Miami, it moved up the Atlantic coast to New York City and across the country to the Midwest. LA kingpins like "Freeway" Rick Ross sold crack cocaine that had been smuggled up through Central America and expanded their Compton-based empires to small cities like Omaha, Nebraska; East Chicago, Illinois; Cincinnati, Ohio; and one day, my own Fort Wayne. Of course, we would later learn the ways that the FBI and CIA were complicit in the proliferation of drugs and guns in our neighborhoods. Then they named the crisis they helped to create the "crack epidemic" and criminalized the black and brown folks (and their babies) who got addicted to crack. But for now, we were just young folks at the crossroads of several major cartels that were building up a thriving business model preying on folks in crippled Rust Belt towns.

Crack hit my family hard. My aunt Marlene, who was my father's sister and my mother's best friend, got caught up in that first wave of users. No one had seen the short- or long-term effects of this new street drug. I remember being at home one day in the winter—

this would have been in the late 80s—and it was cold. We were preparing for the holidays and saw the bad weather coming on the forecast, so we were sticking close to home. Dad had started a fire in our fireplace, and I was sitting right next to it, playing with my Barbie dolls as the heat washed over me. The loud rotary phone on the wall rang, and Dad eased off the floral-printed black couch to answer it. Always a cool character, my father, so when my ears caught his voice reaching higher registers, my attention snapped toward him. It sounded as if the person on the phone was relaying the most absurd news ever. I knew this was serious. My parents were conferring now. Hushed tones. I couldn't make out the words. The adults were masters at keeping things from us children. I strained my ears, trying to make sense of their words. I couldn't. But I could catch it when one of their voices would spike near almost a yell before quieting back down into the hushed whispers whose secrets got trapped inside the walls. Then Dad opened the door and headed out into the freezing winter night. He returned with his sister's three children, my favorite cousins, in tow.

And now, with us kids huddled in my bedroom, I got the story. "Mama on drugs," one cousin said. "It's called crack." Crack. Apparently, my aunt was so hooked on this cheap new drug with a quick high that she was giving away everything she could to get it. My cousins were home alone when their front door was suddenly yanked off its hinges. The landlord, fed up after months and months of my aunt failing to pay rent on the gloomy two-story house, let the winter in, leaving my cousins home alone in the dead cold. They called Dad—my dad, really the only dad they knew—to help them figure out what to do. And it's lucky I liked my cousins, 'cuz we all got a lot of time together after that.

I loved Aunt Marlene too, she was creative and full of spark. She had been accepted into a college art program, but she couldn't pass the gym class needed to get her high school diploma—like a lot of black folk, her fear of swimming was too great. And just like that, a few laps in a pool had changed her life. Aunt Marlene was too much of a carefree spirit to be chained to a machine in an overheated factory, and Fort Wayne didn't really have much else to offer. Crack became her out, I guess. I remember that night so vividly, the first time I really saw the cold wind howling into the fissures in our family. But the drug became familiar. So fast.

Every night on television, we'd see commercials like the 1987 Partnership for a Drug-Free America hot skillet campaign. In thirty seconds, the ad campaign hoped to help America's youth win the war against drugs. "This is drugs," the narrator ominously called out. Then an egg was dropped into the frying pan, and it instantly began to bubble and sizzle and burn on the ends. "This is your brain on drugs. Any questions?" We had to laugh. It was one of the most hilarious things we'd seen on television, and it aired constantly. "Any questions?" we'd say, mocking the narrator's voice, using it as a punch line for jokes we cracked on one another when someone said something stupid. They wanted to scare us straight. The commercial didn't understand how much drug culture was a part of our everyday existence. It wasn't like some stranger in a trench coat was coming up to us offering us crack. No, drug culture was everywhere, from the music we listened to, to the shoes we gave drug names—"check out my new cocaine-white Dopemans"—to the family members who once loved us but now loved the pipe a bit more. Drugs were pernicious in a way that the commercial just didn't get. If someone was handing you a crack pipe, chances were it was a family member or close friend. It wasn't no shadowy stranger trying to fry our brains. People were trying to deal with all kinds of pain and fear and disassociation through the high of drugs and the real economic power of the guns and money, and that is something that the US government, with its jail-them-all approach, did not understand. Those antidrug programs had no idea what was really going on, and it felt like they made little attempt to figure out how to heal our neighborhoods.

My mother was a D.A.R.E. officer, which added another complicated layer to my life. She was *my* D.A.R.E. officer. Every week she'd enter my classroom and teach my peers the eight ways to "Just Say No." We repeated what she taught us, and colored in our D.A.R.E. notebooks and had fun playing Double D.A.R.E., Mom's version of the Nickelodeon show. She was a good teacher. If only life was as easy as a game of Double D.A.R.E. I had friends whose mothers were cleaning drug money for their dealer stepdads and friends whose older brothers were in the game. That was just the shape of their lives, coloring books or no. And if it wasn't already a family business, you could get lured by the promise of wealth. Where else were you gonna get it in Fort Wayne? In a city that didn't have any pipeline to success but the crumbling ladder of factory jobs, my fifth-grade peers were scheming how they could get with this underground market. Here was a career that came with expensive tennis shoes, athletic team apparel, and gold chains, with quick money you could touch and smell and feel, and it didn't feel like tattered work Dickies or smell like machine oil.

Meanwhile, I watched Mom lug that heavy silver drug kit to each of her classes, and then I stared at it sitting in our home every night. It was like a portable drug museum, with cocaine and heroin powder, a chip of crack rock, Quaaludes, and amphetamines, known as "speed." I, too, was trying to balance my intimate ties to the state's antidrug campaign; my vexed relationship with Mom, whose role as drug cop was slowly strangling my social life; and the allure of the street life that surrounded me.

The segregated black neighborhood on the southeast side of Fort Wayne was also sub-segregated into the haves and the have-nots among us black folk. There was a stigma around living in McMillen Park apartments, where Mom and I lived after my parents' divorce, because everyone knew that they were on the cheaper end of housing, even if we didn't have any real understanding of the Section 8 housing system.

But stigma aside, McMillen was one of the most fun places to live. Tons of my school friends lived in the cream-colored Monopoly game piece—looking military fort turned apartments. There were always kids outside to play with. We blasted MC Hammer's *Let's Get It Started* cassette from someone's battery-operated boom box as we made up dance routines in the little patches of grass in front of the apartments. On balmy summer nights, we would stay out way past the streetlights flickering on. Someone would bring a bundle of Fla-Vor-Ice popsicles to share with everyone on the block. We would tear the perforated plastic, fighting to claim the purple or red instead of the green and orange pops. We played tag and hide-and-go-seek, darting in between the rows of our one-story apartments until our armpits were hot and musty. Life in the hood was fun. Sure, there were the occasional fights and the police were called into the maze-like complex quite often, but there was something about living there that felt more genuine and straightforward than the haves side of Village Woods.

The kids in McMillen Park befriended me despite the fact that I was an outsider. Between kindergarten and now I'd been in a different school district. We lived in the front row of apartments, which were slightly better appointed on the outside since they faced the busy intersection of McKinney Avenue and Plaza Drive and sat on a huge "front lawn." I was on the fringes of it all and didn't live as intimately together as my other friends, whose streets were more cramped and gridlocked. Plus, my mom was a cop. Many of my new friends' parents were involved in some kind of criminal activity or another—from drug dealing to numbers running to selling "hot" clothes. And everyone knew we weren't really low-income. We could've left those apartments whenever we wanted and could've even lived "out north" with the white folks.

But Mom wanted to live in the community where she worked the beat. And she wanted me to live among hood kids, like she had, believing it was the only way to keep me humble and grounded and mentally and physically tough. I had to know how to defend myself, and nobody could teach you how to fight like some hood kids. And I could *never* forget that black people around the country were struggling, and the government wasn't doing much to make their situation any better. Mom thought it was her responsibility to share what we had with those in our community. She never wanted there to be a separation between me and the other kids, so she let me play outside with them. And even though I was po-po's daughter, the kids let me in and many even embraced me. By the time we were in middle school, I was just as hood as everybody else in most of the ways that mattered. But Mom never let me go into anyone's house—she didn't want any cause to report someone for whatever type of illegal activity they might be running out of their house. And there was plenty of that.

Because drugs hit McMillen hard. With the drugs came the guns. With the guns came the drugs. And with the poverty and the guns and the drugs, people were starting to say this was gang territory. Land of crack dens. McMillen was a good step above the sho' nuff projects Eden Green and Oaklawn Court deeper into the hood, near the East Central neighborhood, one of the oldest, historically most-segregated areas of our town that black migrants like my grandparents moved into back in the 1950s. Compared to those apartments—gang headquarters and stash houses that attracted a lot of gun violence, slashings, and jumpings—McMillen was projects-light. Drug and gang activity was less conspicuous, and there were more people who were trying to hold down legit low-wage jobs in the retail or fast-food industries, or as attendants at nursing homes and the state school for the developmentally disabled. Nonetheless, Mom got a steep discount on the rent for keeping her squad car parked outside.

At night, I'd be awakened by a *wap, wap, wap*. The first time was enough to send me into Mom's bedroom for safety. It was someone firing off a nine millimeter. Would the morning news report someone getting killed? By the time I was wearing a training bra, my friends and I could differentiate between a nine and a pistol-grip pump or some folks just setting off fireworks. It got to the point where I would hear gunshots in the middle of the night and simply roll over in my bed and wait for silence to lull me back to sleep.

My new life was mirroring the new life of the country. In South Central Los Angeles and Chicago, Folk and People gangs were killing residents who weren't even in the game just because they had on the wrong color in the wrong neighborhood. My friends and me, we lived that history through the music. As part of a peace treaty, some Crips (Folks) and Bloods (People) came together to record an album called *Bangin' on Wax* in 1993. The CPTs in Fort Wayne were fueled by the lyrics of Blood songs like "Piru Love," where Bloody Mary and her crew rapped about shanking Crips with 40 oz. liquor bottles and sending an adversary to his mother's house in a body bag. If I'd wanted, I coulda told my friends all about how I'd been in LA during the height of the gang wars—that was right when I went to visit Aunt Brenda last. Mom was careful to pack mostly neutrals in my miniature suitcase that year. Baldwin Hills, where Aunt Brenda lived, was a bougie enclave, but you never knew what could pop off if we stopped in Compton or Inglewood for some soul food.

And once, when we were all visiting Chicago, I went to the movies with my teenage cousin Terry and one of his Gangster Disciples homeboys, who was wheelchair-bound after taking a couple of bullets in a shootout. The dude was still banging with the Folks even after that, wearing his blue flag and stacking—that's what they called throwing up gang signs—and trying to flirt with Cheri, my pretty older cousin from Cleveland.

My stories of gang culture in the big city weren't even anything to brag about, really. Gangs *were* a big deal but *weren't* a big deal. By the time we were in middle school, they were just a normal part of our lives on the south side of Fort Wayne. I don't know when it became that way. But it feels like one day I looked up and some of the pudgy-faced boys who used to call my Wave Nouveau a Jheri curl were now standing tall alongside their older brothers in the local gangs. The wars never got as bad on our streets as in the metropolises, but Mike Read could tell you that you still betta watch what colors you wear and where you wear them. And like Mom always told me, stray bullets can kill. I saw that too. One night, my friend TJ, the son of a prominent pastor, was sitting in front of the main window at the Old Fort YMCA. That Y was our community center, the black Y. But it also sat right across the street from Eden Green, the heart of gang and drug territory. TJ was fifteen. He and his younger sister were finishing their piano lesson and waiting for their mother, the first lady, to pick them up. Rival gangs started shooting outside. TJ got caught in the crossfire. A bullet pierced his skull and he was rushed to the hospital. Mom heard the call come over her CB. She came into my room and delivered the news: "TJ got shot; they don't know if he's gonna live." I was gutted! *I had just spoken with him right before his lesson.* The first call came from my friend Lori, who had a massive crush on TJ. She could barely talk through her sobs. The phone kept ringing all night, as we patched through three-way calls, the typical "wassup?!" replaced with "Maaaaan, did you hear about TJ?" We prayed for days that TJ would live.

He didn't die. He would live, they said, probably with blindness and brain damage. But somehow, TJ escaped those fates too. The Christian community was praising the miraculous power of the Lord for months after the shooting. His doctors thought it best to leave the bullet in his brain. TJ would walk around for the rest of his life with that bullet as his testimony of the day he almost died but Jesus had other plans.

It seemed like daily somebody else in my grade was joining a gang. I didn't know what the gangs were *doing* besides throwing up their signs—which I used to practice in the mirror at home but wouldn't dare do in front of one of them—occasionally jumping folks, and posting up at the skating rink. The gangstas' actual job, which I was barely aware of as a kid, was to provide the muscle for the local drug trade, move weight, enforce payment. Crack was ever present in my life, and so were gangs, but I never quite made the connection between the two. As an adult, I would come to see that all us kids growing up were at the mercy of this larger force in ways we couldn't even imagine at the time.

Some of us were tapped to join gangs. It was mostly boys, plus some of the cute girls who already had an older brother or cousin in the gang, or kids who you knew were heading toward trouble because they had already done a stint or two at Sol A. Wood Youth Center—"Sollywood" in my dad's days there. With the colors and the hand signs and the camaraderie, a gang looked like a place you could *belong*. It seemed like the fraternities and sororities at Indiana University that Mom was always talking about, or a recreational group for wayward teens that was a little scary to get "jumped into" but then was all matching outfits and special privileges. Except for the stabbings and beatings. Or the more rare murders. Or the time that the CPTs threatened to kill a cop on New Year's Eve, a night my mother was scheduled to work her beat overtime. I sat on her bed as she adjusted and readjusted the straps on her Kevlar bullet-proof vest. Yeah, the gangs seemed real cool to preteen me sometimes, one of several groups of idolizable teenagers flashing their color-coordinated Dopemans and their tight social bonds at the skating rink. But sometimes it was like sitting on the bed waiting for Mom to return home, or by the phone, waiting for a phone call about a friend in the hospital.

The night Mike got jumped, I had come dressed like Shalonna and Courtney, two of the coolest, prettiest, and most popular eighth-grade girls at my school. For some reason, they saw fit to let me, a sixth grader, join their clique. We called ourselves "The Ronis," after singer Bobby Brown's hit slow jam "Tenderoni." We planned it out in school: we would each pick a "roni" name and get it airbrushed in our favorite color down the front of the left leg of a pair of light-wash jeans. This wasn't an easy time for me with Mom; we were circling around and around each other, always ready to pop off. But it was times like this that I loved her so much, because she understood the stakes without me even having to explain to her why it mattered that two older girls seemed to genuinely like me and wanted to bring me into their crew. To show up at all-night skating without the airbrushed jeans would've been social suicide.

So Mom gave me some money and dropped me off at the mall so I could get my jeans airbrushed. She'd pay for the airbrush as long as I supplied my own jeans, she said. Fair enough. When I rolled up to the girls in the center of the rink, Shalonna and Courtney were kind of shocked that I'd actually followed through. And the girls in my grade were shocked (and probably a lil' salty) by the fact that Shalonna and Courtney let me dress like them. I got "Mac-A-Roni" in turquoise airbrush. On the eve of thirteen and I already saw myself as a playgirl, a mack mama, the female counterpart to Kris Kross's Mac Daddy and Daddy Mac. It was all so ephemeral, so in the moment. The airbrush could instantly transform an old pair of jeans, and that's what fashion was for, to remake something old into something *fresh*.

If fashion told everyone who you were, shoes were a big part of it. And tennis shoes were *the* shoe in the skating rink. Crazy, right? You only had them on for the first few minutes before storing them away in a locker. But then two a.m. would roll around and the center of the rink became a dance floor. Shalonna, Courtney, and I ran back to the lockers to grab our shoes, and *now* our matching airbrushed jeans outfits were complete. Your shoe game had to be tight. Even if we were wearing the cheapest shoe that maker sold, it was still important that they were clean and that they matched the 'fit. Each of us girls ran to grab the cutie we'd been eying all night and take him onto the dance floor. Shalonna grabbed one of Mike Read's friends, a light-skinned boy named Lonnie, who she had recently started *talkin'* to.

For me, it was Tony, a light-skinned boy with almond-shaped eyes and curly hair—features that supported his claim that he was mixed Korean and black. Tony wore his hair in a popular men's haircut called a bob and was a fly dresser, always crisp and clean. This night he had on a gray sweatshirt with a neatly pressed crease down the middle—as sharp as the ones on his dark-wash jeans— which he removed to reveal a red t-shirt. He sported a pair of white leather Dopemans with a black swoosh. I glimpsed at and then slightly stumbled over them at the same time as he pulled me into him, closer than usual. Tony and I made it a point to dance together at least once per party, but we knew it could never amount to anything because he went to a different school and was gang-affiliated. With me being "Five-0"'s daughter (the nickname we gave to cops because of the old TV show *Hawaii Five-0*), that just wouldn't be a good look for him. So we lived in that moment of rhythmic slow grinding as R&B crooner Keith Sweat whined, "*How deep is your love*." I laid my face in the crook of Tony's neck, the scent of his Cool Water cologne blighting out the thick smell of sweaty gym socks that hovered in the air around us like a nosy chaperone.

The skating rink allowed for this kind of intimacy between kids who were in gangs and those who weren't, more so than any other space in town. Parents didn't want their "good" kids affiliating with gangsters, but the skating rink was considered neutral ground, a space for good, clean fun, despite the fact that Roller Dome South was mostly CPT territory. The Cs would congregate down at the end of the row of felt-covered benches that lined the east side of the rink, where the light was dim and they could clock everyone entering and exiting. You felt their presence. Elementary-aged kids learned to stay out of their way and have as little direct contact as possible. But skating rinks being the social spaces that they are, you do end up talking to folks and developing crushes on some of the boys and worshipping some of the gang queens, wishing you could be as fly or skate as well as some of them. Each year, from the time I was in second grade till sixth grade, I would inch my way closer to their circle, just hanging right on the periphery of danger, close enough to hear their conversations and get a whiff of their cologne-drenched bodies. Some of these guys, like Duron Martin and Lil Tanky Jones and Marty B., had become thug celebrities. None of the core dudes ever said much to me other than that I had pretty eyes, on account that they knew who my mother was.

Most of those boys had at least one pair of Dopemans. They seemed to be standard-issue dope boy attire, in basic colors like white on black or black on white, red, or navy with the gleaming white Nike swoosh. Whether leather or nylon or suede, the shoes were always *fresh to death*. Not high quality, but high on the desire charts. All of our favorite West Coast rappers and East Coast b-boys were wearing them. And by the early 90s, so were we, because they were durable and cheap, something that made sense to our frugal parents (not that my mom could ever be called frugal).

Nike was actually a no-name shoe company before it launched the Dopemans, or Cortez, during the height of the 1972 Summer Olympics. It was a track-and-field shoe specially designed to fill a gap in the market. Bill Bowerman, a track-and-field coach at the University of Oregon and an Olympic trainer, worked with engineers to create the original prototype for the Cortez in 1968. They needed a shoe that was super lightweight but that was durable enough to protect from road shock. The heel had to have enough padding to protect the Achilles tendon from fatigue and strain, which could lead to injury. Bowerman tinkered with the shoe for four years as he and his business partner, Phil Knight, exhausted all of their resources to keep the business afloat until the shoe was ready for launch. The pair was not prepared for the success of the Cortez, which vaulted to fame through smart marketing that caught and rode the wave of public attention on Olympic track and field. The Cortez grossed nearly $5 million (in today's figures) in sales mere months after it was released. It was the company's crown jewel. Nike invested millions to enhance the Cortez in those early years, swapping the heavier leather for a lighter nylon-and-suede combo.

By the time I was entering adolescence in the late 1980s, the Cortez had lost a lot of its luster, but none of its staying power. By that point, Nike was in the basketball shoe game and the Air Jordan and Air Force 1 reigned supreme, and Nike had plenty of newer track shoe designs on offer. But Cortez sales remained consistent because they were rebranded as a lifestyle shoe, endorsed by blond bombshell Farrah Fawcett, who had sported a pair of the red, white, and blue classic Cortezes on the set of *Charlie's Angels*. In the early 1990s, the brand tapped megastar Whitney Houston, the vocal pop powerhouse who had been branded to *transcend* race, to endorse the shoe. She paired the classic Cortez with a white, red, and blue track suit during her moving rendition of the national anthem at Super Bowl XXV, just after the United States had entered the First Gulf War. Both Fawcett and Houston projected the right lifestyle for the shoe, and they had young, adoring suburban fan bases that would beg their parents to buy them the shoes. But Nike was smart enough to recognize the hip hop zeitgeist, so they didn't stick with just their suburban market. N.W.A. front man Eric "Eazy-E" Wright made Nike apparel and shoes part of his brand, and Nike capitalized on the new look. It's hard to imagine now what an insightful move that was.

I had the biggest crush on Eazy-E. He was a pint-size dope-boy-turned-rapper with a high-pitched voice and a dry Jheri curl. That combination was wack on the guys I saw walking around Fort Wayne. But Eazy-E had charm and charisma and confidence . . . and MONEY. And I knew N.W.A.'s entire catalogue. The Fort Wayne library was oddly hip, and they had all of N.W.A.'s music on cassette. I would use my library card to check out the tapes and then dub them using my dual-cassette stereo. This was one of those moments where being a nerd paid off. While my friends were paying full price for all of N.W.A.'s music, I was getting it for free. I would listen for hours as Eazy-E and Ice Cube and MC Ren rapped about street life, hustling, and racist cops. When I was mad at my mother, I would blast "Fuck the Police"—when she wasn't home, of course. I delved into Eazy-E's world of Compton as I stared at the cover art. N.W.A. always wore something basic: LA Raiders jackets with white Nike t-shirts or sweatshirts with a black Nike swoosh. Eazy was usually in black Dopemans with a white swoosh or sometimes the white-on-white ones.

By solidifying what seemed like a partnership with Eazy-E, Nike embraced street culture in a way that no other brand had at the time. Adidas had a relationship with Queens-based Run DMC, Troop with LL Cool J, and British Knights with MC Hammer, but their images were wholesome compared to the content N.W.A. was producing: the overt dope dealing, wild sex, and gun violence. Of course, Nike didn't do this out of love for black kids like me. They went for the profit, knowing that hood kids and white kids in the suburbs wanted to look like their rap idols. And they for damn sure weren't showing up on our doorsteps to give their condolences to so-and-so's mama after her kid was gunned down in their shoes or beaten and robbed for them. But something about their acknowledgment of our culture felt like they understood us, they saw the emerging tidal force that was *our* hip hop culture. They picked the blackest, most foulmouthed rapper to endorse their shoes—alongside the reigning princess of pop, Whitney Houston, and the white lady.

Now, structurally, a pair of Cortez and a pair of Dopemans are the same shoe. But to my mind they have different DNA. The man who sold drugs in our neighborhood, the dope dealer, the dope man, or the "d-boy," for short, wore those shoes, or at least in our minds he did. We knew him. Yeah, he had some menacing ways, but he wasn't separate from us. He was our uncles, older brothers, the dude whose social world we orbited at the skating rink, wishing we could date him but knowing we didn't want to go through the violence or the bother of being jumped in by the girls in the gang in order to have a chance to get him. These men were fly. They were the ones who rarely returned our love or showed up at our special functions. They were the ones with whom we took Polaroid pictures when we visited them in the *pen*. They were the ones who died too soon and whose blood we cleaned out of their clothes. And something about their style rang true. It was something to emulate and desire. In hindsight, I don't know why I ever thought Nike would actually name one of its shoes Dopemans, but at the time I did, never even questioning it; it was because of N.W.A.

When N.W.A. released "Dope Man" in 1987, they put to music what we knew. In the song, crack fiends were yelling after the dope man, trying to get their next high: *"Dope man, please can I have another hit?"* Women called "strawberries" were willing to *"sell pussy for crack."* The infectious chorus *"Dope man! Dope man!,"* chanted over a bass-laden Dr. Dre beat, was easy for us to recite. In environments where we were all disenfranchised, the dope man had a degree of power and autonomy, even though he, too, was subject to getting cracked over the head by a rogue cop's billy club. The N.W.A. song and others like it, including their 1988 follow-up "Gangsta Gangsta," gave the gangsta a persona. Part reality, part mythical, it allowed us to not focus so much on the dope boys and gangstas who were running roughshod in our apartment complex or the dudes who were getting my aunties and family friends strung out. All of a sudden we could see them as pseudo-heroic figures who repped our hoods and our culture for the world. We wanted them to win, to elude the racist cops.

These narratives, built around things of beauty, objects of desire that hip hop culture brought us, put a sort of needed filter on the harsh realities of the world represented in the music. On the one hand, we saw our relatives, loved ones we'd looked up to, cracked out, eyes wide like saucers, loud when they weren't supposed to be. Skinny. Teeth yellow, skin sallow. And all across our neighborhood we saw how one family member on crack became an indictment of the entire family. "So-and-so's mama's on crack," you would hear. On the other hand, hip hop allowed us to laugh at our pain. Miami bass rap group the Dogs released their song "Crack Rock" in 1990, with a hook of elementary-school-aged kids chanting "*Na, na, na, na, na, your mama's on crack rock!*" over an 808-laced beat while the girl on the receiving end of the taunt chanted back things like "*You got my mama bent!*" and "*Yours is too!*" That song was excruciating in its comedy because that situation was so real for so many of us. Hardly anyone, even in the better parts of the black side of town, could boast that not one of their relatives was strung out. But even still, we would run up to people and yell the song's hook in their faces. That was one of the ways we coped.

Our gang-inspired fashion spoke to a painful truth: we had an intimacy with crack cocaine that we couldn't escape. The loss of factory-funded middle-class culture was devastating for folks who had derived their entire sense of worth from being a bigwig in the factory. We watched as our parents' freedom dreams morphed into crack vapor. Each tug on the pipe made the future look grim for the baby boomers. We kids felt the brunt of it. More and more of our loved ones, those charged with protecting us and making a better life for us, took to the crack pipe to blight out their troubles. They didn't know the effects of crack, the short-term ones, where the chemical dependency makes crack exponentially more addictive than heroin, or the long-term, how that substance created a generation of addicts and tore apart families. But this crazy, horrifying, infuriating, heartbreaking history that fellow Rust Belt kid, Chicago native Kanye West, tells in his song "Crack Music" also brought with it a wave of creative cultural expression that took on enormous momentum and power. The music, the fashion, the culture I grew up with united me with my peers, and does still. And I, a kid of the crack era, am forced to wrestle with these contradictions, even as I glorify the Dopemans name we gave the Nike Cortez.

5

Baggy Jeans

Thud-THUD, thud-THUD. I could hear my feet hitting the concrete heavy, clocking my exhaustion in the weight of my cadence. I had run from the cluster of dorms in the center of campus, past Library Pond, and was now at the base of a long cement strip that led up to my dorm, Kehaya House, on the fringes of campus. I could see the massive bay windows of Kehaya, nicknamed "Kehyatt" on account of it looking like a fancy beach resort, especially compared to the Gothic architecture of some of the other dorms that firmly situated you in New England. My fatigued muscles felt like warm, lactic acid–flavored Jell-O. I had one hand gripping the waistband of my oversize lime-green BOSS jeans (a men's 36 that drowned my rail-thin body), as the other pumped wildly trying to help me propel my body up the slight incline. *Why the hell did Kehaya have to be so far from everything?* This was a problem for me, someone who was always almost late for curfew.

As usual, I had stuck around after dinner, flitting and bopping around the various dorms my friends lived in instead of settling down at the desk in my room to study. So I was now in a race against the clock. I had learned so much about church bells since moving from my black-ass middle school in Fort Wayne to St. Paul's, a preppy-ass boarding school in Concord, New Hampshire, earlier that year. Our daily lives were ordered around those bells. The clock had struck nine p.m., but I still had twelve dings of the clock gong to make it in the door before I was technically late, something for which I was increasingly grateful. And I pushed that limit many nights, especially on the weekends.

I made it on the tenth ding and opened the wide wooden door that felt especially heavy now—panting and heaving—to hear my house advisor Mrs. Branson say in a kind yet firm voice, "Cutting it close again, Tanisha." "I know. I'm sorry Mrs. Branson," I said, flashing her a toothy smile. "It won't happen again." We both knew it would. I was away from home for the first time at fifteen, experiencing the sort of freedom that I had dreamed of but really couldn't have imagined a year earlier when I went to my parents and told them I wanted to go to boarding school, more than eight hundred miles away from home, no less.

But more than being late and more than being away from home, what I remember most is those baggy jeans. My shockingly loud jeans connected me with my new black friends at St. Paul's, who were from cool places like Brooklyn, Yonkers, Roxbury, and Philly. We all had different vantage points and connections to hip hop culture. But our baggy jeans spoke a common language, one that rooted us black teens—mostly from poor and working-class families on the fringes—in a community of young folks struggling to eke out a voice in a world that constantly showed it didn't love us. On campus, we communed, locating a safe space in the music and the fashion culture it was spawning against the backdrop of this posh private school, the playground of the white and privileged, this place that seemed to ooze old money—from the built environment to the Mary Janes and wool shift dresses and blazers. We were style rebels whose baggy jeans and oversize-t-shirt-clad bodies served as emblems of the larger moment we were living through—which has now come to be known as the golden era of hip hop.

Oh, the golden era. That time between the late 1980s and the mid-1990s when hip hop was feeling itself, expanding exponentially, shape-shifting, taking up space, asserting its staying power. Artists like A Tribe Called Quest, De La Soul, Queen Latifah, Monie Love, Jungle Brothers, X Clan, Public Enemy, Rakim, EPMD, Big Daddy Kane, Digable Planets, Kwamé, Gang Starr, The Pharcyde, Leaders of the New School, Brand Nubian, and Hieroglyphics were in steady rotation. They were brash innovators with music tech, transporting the house party from Anyhood, USA, to distant regions of the diaspora, connecting us sonically to our African roots. And the fashion was just as daring as the music itself—the ankhs, headdresses, baggy jeans, bright colors, polka dots—graffitiing our identity as the hip hop generation onto our melanated flesh.

In the early 1990s in particular, there was a flourish of hip hop–inspired fashion lines, from Cross Colours and Karl Kani to FUBU and Walker Wear. Many of those brands patterned themselves after Ralph Lauren (Polo), selling an urban lifestyle as much as the garments themselves. Girls were wearing these lines too, with legends like TLC, Aaliyah, and Mary J. Blige serving as our muses; suddenly, being a tomboy was acceptable in my hometown. The mainstream fashion industry was clamoring to name our style so they could cash in on our desire, our love of excess. They ended up settling for "gang wear" and "urban wear." Yeah, those fashion industry insiders didn't even try to hide their racial biases toward the black folks they were capitalizing on. Whatever; it was still our fashion, and we was fresh dipped, fly from head to toe in the baggiest of clothes in the most ostentatious colors.

These clothes felt like they could speak for me. I was a black girl who was part of this culture, and had been for years at this point. Now black fashion designers had etched out space to make us visible where previously we had been ignored. So when I trekked off to boarding school, it didn't even occur to me that I should pack anything other than the garments in my closet—like these baggy jeans that kept making my life logistically difficult in my nightly race against the old chapel clock, but also made me feel the most rooted and connected to myself. One of the biggest struggles for kids like me coming straight out of our communities and into the yuppie-in-training world of elite boarding schools is that nothing you've experienced up to that point can prepare you for entering that space. You bring all of your stuff—your clothes and your culture and your emotional baggage—from home. You wear it like a comfort blanket. The space wants to yank it away, expose you, shame you, and then re-dress you in the clothes it deems fit.

My parents were more supportive than I thought they'd be when I came to them with my desire to go to boarding school. I'd gotten the idea from my big cousin Jonathan, who would graduate from St. Paul's the year before I arrived. Mom was all for me going to a boarding school, in my mind, mostly because she wanted me out of her house. She took me school shopping, which was a way for her to communicate in her own love language that she was proud of me, wanted me to succeed in every way, and that she'd miss me.

Mom and I went to every bargain store from Value City to Wal-Mart to cobble together my new wardrobe. Oversize lumberjack flannels and sweaters from the men's department in gray and burgundy and navy blue. Knockoff Timberlands (which I think said "Timber*line*," or some such, on the label). Jeans in every color, snatched from a sale rack. The school's dress code banned classic blue jeans in class and in chapel, but Jonathan had told me that there was a loophole: you could wear *colored* jeans. They didn't see us coming in our Crayola crayon box of denim jeans when they wrote "blue jeans" into that dress code. It was a stroke of black kid genius, the sort of ingenuity that sparked hip hop culture to begin with. This is how I was able to rock my lime-green BOSS jeans in algebra and biology class, puttin' a little swag in my step as I awkwardly strutted from classroom to classroom while trying to hold up those jeans, book bag in tow.

My dad wasn't so thrilled about his baby girl wanting to go so far away, but he was all for the fact that I'd be getting the type of education that his Alabama migrant parents could've only dreamed of and brushing shoulders with some of the brightest students in the world. Since preschool, he had made me study the dictionary and do summer reading programs and attend enrichment camps. I took the SAT for the first time when I was twelve. My older godbrother, who had taken to calling me "Urkel" (after the beloved nerd Steve Urkel on *Family Matters*), and his high school friends were standing in line with me to take the test asking, "Urkel, what *you* doing here?!"

Everything in my life seemed to have prepared me for this moment. And truth be told, I was trying to go to boarding school to get away from Fort Wayne just as much (and probably more, if I'm being honest) as I was in search of a good education. I mean, the curriculum at Village Woods *was* lackluster. Our school was underfunded, we had old, outdated textbooks, and the teachers were overworked and woefully underpaid. That's how they did the predominantly black schools. I knew enough to know that there was a better education to be had out there. So at St. Paul's I could find both social sanctuary and a high-quality education.

My parents worked with the financial aid office to make the jaw-dropping $18,000 per year cost of attendance affordable (now St. Paul's is $60,000 per year), and one of my favorite teachers, Mr. Kreamer, created an individualized English literature curriculum to get me up to speed for my application. My classmates would be like, "Yo, Mr. Kreamer, why Tanisha not doin' what we doin'?" But they already thought I was a super nerd by that point anyway, so they weren't shocked when I told them I was heading to a special school. Some even wore it as a badge of honor, sorta like *my* winning was a win for us *all*. I appreciated that about my friends.

So I packed up my bags in Fort Wayne, Indiana, and I unpacked them in Concord, New Hampshire. I had made it out of my rusty, dusty town and into one of the so-called elite sixteen boarding schools—so named because they were the most expensive, rigorous, and selective schools in the country. This place had educated members of old-money families such as the Vanderbilts and the Pillsburys (yep, the Pillsbury Doughboy folks)—though much of this prestige mess was lost on me at the time.

Initially, what impressed *me* was the chance to remake myself. Of course, at St. Paul's I was immediately known as "Johnny Glover's cousin." But I was cool with that. My cousin Jonathan—no one in our family had *ever* referred to him as Johnny—was *the man* at St. Paul's. Girls thought he was fine; guys envied his physique, charisma, and unassuming brilliance. He was off at Dartmouth College now, but according to the older kids, he had left instructions: be nice to my cousin . . . and don't you dare try to holla at her!

They at least heeded the first part of his instructions. When I arrived, folks of all races rolled out the welcome wagon for me. I wore the title "Johnny Glover's cousin" with pride. It was much, *much* better than being "Officer Ford's daughter," which I had come to despise. Both my relatives cast long shadows, but Mom's seemed to suck the entire community in to surveil and police my behavior, whereas being Johnny Glover's cousin came with nothing but social cachet, something that I, a girl who had become accustomed to being popular, craved.

I was starting to catch my breath now as I made my way up Kehaya House's massive open staircase, rubbing my hand along the smooth blond wood of the railing as I yelled out to a few of the girls in my form I was friendly with, "Wassup, Sam! Heyyy, Sarah!" They were sitting downstairs in the lounge area working on a group project, something I should have been doing, but at the time, I saw St. Paul's as a glorified summer camp, the best possible form of glamping. I was used to being at the top of my class back home; I wasn't worried about it. Then, reality struck. This was an institution with a learning curve so steep that I couldn't even see how close I was to crashing until I received my first term grades (which landed me on academic probation).

I could hear my voice echoing through the halls as I made my greetings in the building, which was typically pretty quiet after dinner. Study hours. Hearing the sound of my own voice, thick with hood colloquialisms, ricocheting off the walls, was a reminder of the many ways I still felt like I didn't quite belong here, the glamorous "Johnny Glover's cousin" label be damned. At St. Paul's, incubator for America's elite, being loud was a sign of poor social grooming. I was one of only three black girls in my dorm (and one of maybe twenty black girls in our entire school of slightly more than five hundred) and the only hood girl. The other two would have been considered *Oreos* (black on the outside, white on the inside) back at home, but here, they were "well-adjusted" and "socially prepared." I couldn't really get with this new social order at St. Paul's.

At home, we were all loud and boisterous. Everything happened at maximum decibels: we listened to our music loud, cracked jokes loud, and wore loud clothes, like the lime-green pants I was currently draped in. And it never occurred to me that there was anything wrong with that. You had to be loud at home in order to be seen, heard, respected. So that's how I had learned to function in the world. My family was loud, my friends were loud. Hell, even the white folks were loud, especially when the bigots were yelling racial epithets like "Nigger Go Home!" That was a totally normal thing to hear when I stepped outside of the black community in Fort Wayne and dared to eat or play—or go to school—in a neighborhood where blacks weren't welcome. This vigilante policing of racial boundaries in my hometown made it so I could never forget that racism was real.

At St. Paul's though, that sort of overt racism wasn't the norm. Any anti-black or -brown sentiment was generally masked by a smug upper-crust New England–ness that thought itself too refined and restrained to emote something as guttural as the white folks back home did. The white students who attended were about as diverse in origin stories as the black and brown kids—with some of these white kids coming from dirt-poor, socially unimportant families from towns that lacked the luster of a Greenwich, Connecticut. But at first they all melted together into a pool of wealthy whiteness in my mind. In other words, for me class status or the performance of status through certain social "graces" came to be the way I separated the haves (whites) from the have-nots (black and brown folks). And there were some black and Asian and Latino haves. But they mostly performed the same understated behavior as the wealthy white folks.

Class status. It was something I had never even considered growing up. I knew some people had better toys or better stereo equipment and Discmans and clothes and shoes than others, but I had never thought about differences in socioeconomic status or the power and influence that came with being upper class. Nor did I realize how class status informed folks' social behaviors, especially not black folks. All the black people I knew basically acted the same, spoke the same, and were pretty much of the same class status: poor or one paycheck from it. I didn't know real-life black people like the bougie Bankses on *The Fresh Prince of Bel-Air*. They were mostly a television fiction to me. Sure, there were a couple of kids we called Oreos, but even their behavior looked nothing like what I saw on my new campus.

Very few things here at St. Paul's were spoken out loud. Most of the indoctrination to this place came through whispers. For example, no one told me I was dressed inappropriately. I mean, technically, everything I wore fit the dress code. But my roommate and the other girls in my dorm who either came from upper-class families or who had been attending these elite private institutions since grade school clearly knew a different script. I learned for the first time about brands such as Ann Taylor, J. Crew, and L.L.Bean. And Ralph Lauren. I recognized Ralph Lauren. We simply called the brand "Polo" back home. I wore Polo—including a $200 pair of wire-rimmed glasses; a real upgrade from my first no-name-brand pair. My friends and I would buy everything oversize (often knockoff Polo from the Korean flea market) to get the same effect as the clothes Cross Colours and other black-owned labels were making, and we'd rock Polo from head to toe, with the guys and hard-core tomboys even showing off the elastic waistband of their Polo draws. To wealthy white folks, this was a gratuitous display. These prep school girls wore Polo a completely different way. For most of them, the Ralph Lauren brand represented the restraint of white East Coast high society with its equestrian sports, high tea, and yachting. They wore the clothes in muted colors, without the brand name all over everything. Nah son, that's just not what we was doing with Polo, or with the "urban" brands.

Baggy jeans brands like Cross Colours appealed to us precisely because they were loud, in color and in shape, and had the brand logos stitched or screen printed all over them. In 1989, Carl Jones launched Cross Colours, his fashion love letter to the hip hop generation—to those of us who were making statements out of baggy jeans because we had to wear ill-fitting hand-me-down pants and work with what we had. Jones was inspired by the black kids he saw riding the New York City subway in their oversize jeans that hung with a sag. Long before they had a name that inspired awe and could be sold at an inflated price point, oversize jeans had represented a condition, a socioeconomic status. Some have even said it's a mindset. Jones took that shame and spun it into fashion gold, a rainbow of black pride with a political message, by taking the hand-me-down jean and rebranding it and giving it the name "baggy." Baggy jeans. They were my generation's zoot suit, all cool and rebellious and style-forward.

These St. Paul's girls, on the other hand, had been conditioned into wearing quiet clothes—polite shift dresses in muted tones, chunky Mary Janes, black cocktail dresses, modest jewelry, their hair either tucked into a neat bun or (even when it was down and hanging loose) with a tamed quality that wasn't so easy for us black girls, who were away from our braiders and beauticians, to achieve. And the more formal events on campus were designed for you to need this type of attire in order to feel like you fit the occasion.

One such event was Seated Meal, a formal dining experience held a dozen times throughout the year that matched students of various forms and houses with several faculty members. I remember going to my first Seated Meal in a scoop-neck, striped, fitted shirt and a shabby skirt, one of the few bottoms I owned at the time that was *not* baggy jeans. There was so much silverware! I didn't know where or how to start. And then the faculty member appointed to my table launched in: "So, Tanisha, how are you finding St. Paul's?," with an air that translated in my ears as sophisticated and erudite. And I realized that nothing in my life experience had prepared me to *conversate* with stuffy white male prep school teachers. More than anything, I was tacitly shown that it was better to at least *look* the part as I figured out all the uppity class bullshit. So I called Mom one night, in a panic after one Seated Meal, like: "Mom, these girls, they dress completely different. I hate their look; it's so preppy!" And in the same breath, I begged her to buy me some of those boring clothes.

Never one to let her daughter go without, *especially* in front of *dicty* white folk, Mom hooked me up over Thanksgiving break with some shift dresses from Casual Corner and a couple of the white button-down blouses the girls wore underneath. I also picked out two pairs of Nine West chunky-heeled Mary Janes, in black and brown, from JCPenney. And, of course, opaque tights. I can't quite explain how crucial those tights were to a look. The girls wore them in gray, black, and brown, sometimes with subtle ribbing, nothing too racy, of course. Those tights were the key to a polished look. I still own tons of those tights to this day; I drank the Kool-Aid.

So my wardrobe and I were both starting to get the hang of it here now. I breezed down one of the main corridors on my way to my room on the second floor, throwing out more "wassups!" as I peeked my head in on one of my favorite sixth formers, Erika. She was a super down-to-earth, athletic white girl who seemed to navigate St. Paul's well without getting caught up in the pretension of it all. We bonded after she let me butcher her hair with a pair of kitchen shears. I really thought I could cut it! After all, I had been cutting, relaxing, and styling my own hair since I was twelve. I even brought out my relaxer one time and schooled some of the girls who came from other black and brown hoods on the peptide-bond science of black hair care. Alas, I quickly learned when I made my first slice into Erika's back-length, straight, wheat-blonde hair that this type of hair cuts completely differently. I should've stopped then, but my ego wouldn't let me. Fortunately, Mel, a leggy redhead from a suburb of Boston, finally rescued Erika from my hack job (after admonishing us for using kitchen shears for a haircut in the first place), which left her with a very short bob. And, even after all of that, Erika still liked me; she always looked out for me.

My roommate was a Korean-American girl named Juli. Juli came from a boarding school–type family, so she knew the ropes well, and played her position consistently: the best way to make friends was to always have sugary snacks like powdered donuts on hand. That meant there was always a stream of people coming in and out of our room. Something I quickly tired of. Juli loved movie and Broadway play soundtracks. Since she was practically always there, pulling her social circle into orbit around her donuts, and I was always out *in them streets* with my social circle being across campus where all the black and brown folks lived, she usually controlled the music in our room. She played the *Beaches* soundtrack on repeat. By the end of the first quarter, I knew all the songs by heart, and we would do our best Bette Midler impressions together in the morning as we shrugged off our bathrobes and dressed and combed our hair to head out to morning chapel: "*Do you buy a titsling or do you buy a brassieeeeeere?!*"

But no one was in our room tonight, not even Juli. Silence. Solitude. *My turn to listen to my music on speakers instead of headphones.*

I stepped up into the seat of our huge bay window—even standing full up with my arms outstretched, the window was way taller than me—and pressed my face up against the glass, looking out over the path that led out of the thicket of trees that I had just run through in order to make it here before curfew. My mind drifted to home. I was more homesick than I wanted to admit to myself. I was keeping in touch with a couple of friends through the occasional letter or as much time on the pay phone as I could get before some other girl banged on the glass for her turn. Two phones for thirty girls meant that you never talked to anyone long. But hearing Shante or Zeke or Ayesha's voice for even a few minutes was enough to send me into an emotional spiral of home-induced illness. I had fought so hard to be free of that steel prison—the place that killed dreams. I had achieved so much and run so far, and here I had a creative outlet to imagine endless possibilities for my life, and now all I wanted was to hear someone speak that up-South Fort Wayne drawl and tell me some basic story about some dude I used to like.

I marched up the stairs in our luxury loft suite to my sleeping quarters. I turned on the small black Sony boom box that sat on my nightstand and popped in Aaliyah's CD. I skipped to track six and allowed Aaliyah's rendition of the Isley Brothers' "At Your Best (You Are Love)" to wash over me, sonic salve for my melancholy. I remembered how much Dad had loved Aaliyah's pure and clear vocals on the track when I played it for him when he came up to visit for parents' weekend. "*Let me knoooow, let me knooooow-oh . . .*" I soaked in this moment of solace.

My mind drifted to Mom, wondering what she was doing now that she was a premature empty nester. Things between Mom and me had become super strained by the time I was wrapping up middle school. Mom had taken a position in the detective bureau, working sex crimes cases. Being a detective came with a certain type of prestige, for sure, but it was emotionally wrenching work. Most of her cases involved assaults against children, some of them her former D.A.R.E. students and their families. Mom would come home every day emotionally spent. Her once optimistic outlook was darkened by her window-seat view of the vilest human acts imaginable, her concern for her child victims, and her dismay that she couldn't save them all. She wore this burden like a rubber tire around her neck—it was heavy and unwieldy, nearly impossible to throw off. She would stop home to shed the suit and dressy loafers that had now replaced her police uniform as her daily work attire, staying just long enough to yell at me for not cleaning the house properly . . . or for breathing, it felt like. She'd change into her old uniform. And then she was off to one of her part-time security gigs.

I was raised not to talk back to adults, but hell, I was almost an adult by then anyway, or at least it felt like it. I was home alone so much by this point, and had been for most of middle school, that I made all of my own meals, and even food for Mom—elaborate dinners like fried chicken or fish, macaroni and cheese, crescent rolls and green beans, and layered cakes and frosted sugar cookies. I washed all of my own clothes, made my own schedule, disciplined myself to sit down to do homework each night, and often put myself to bed before Mom got home from her second job or one of the college classes she was taking to finish her bachelor's degree.

I knew she was working hard. She showed it in the stuff she could buy me: a Honda Elite moped, the latest cordless phone, a fancy Casio keyboard, and a sleek new bedroom set. I had every material thing I could want, but what I wanted most was her. Her love and attention. Like it used to be back when she and Dad were still married, when it felt like there was so much love to go around, when I would fall asleep nested between their two warm bodies. And with Mom taking in every black girl or family member in the neighborhood who needed refuge, guidance, or mentorship, it felt like there was never anything left over for me, or my problems—some of them hauntingly dark. I needed a mom too. We were trapped between her professional exhaustion and my teenage melancholy, which was becoming increasingly unbearable for Mom. We didn't have any sort of counseling or support to help us figure out our own baggage. The only thing I could think to do was flee. And the only way I knew how to do it was with my smarts.

I made it to the end of my Aaliyah song without someone asking me to turn it down. Typically, when I played my music—Soul for Real's "Candy Rain" or Pete Rock & C. L. Smooth's "They Reminisce Over You (T.R.O.Y.)"—either Juli or one of our suitemates, Laurel and Rebecca, would come in to tell me to turn it down. They were polite enough, but damn, it was as if black music sounded louder to them than the rock and punk music they blasted on the regular. These days we'd call that microaggression.

When I first got there, the south side girl in me used to pop off. Constantly! There was this one obnoxious white girl named Hannah whose main purpose, I swear, was to find a way to get me kicked out of school. She alleged that I stole one of her art projects in our Visual Design class. We were all working on the same thing: three-dimensional shapes. Everyone's looked alike, and she and I both forgot to put our names on them. I picked hers up by accident. And all of a sudden what should have just been one third former asking another third former if they had mistakenly picked up the wrong project turned into her reporting me to the administration, which prompted some administrator to send two sixth-form black girls, Shayla and Tonya, who lived in Hannah's dorm, over to talk to me. Again one of those "polite" ways that rich folks go about solving problems. Folks in the hood have way simpler, way more direct methods for handling shit. I still believe that to this day. Apparently, the school recognized the racial optics of it all and thought it best to handle it in this more "informal" way (sending black teenage girls to do its bidding), especially for Johnny Glover's cousin.

Again, the drawing assignment issue seemed so basic to me that it didn't have to come to all of this. But the black girls told me this dry snitching Hannah was intimidated by me. Apparently, my baggy jeans and "Brandy braids" screamed *ghetto queen* and, although she was totally taller and bigger than me, *she* was the intimidated one. She struck me as one of those wealthy three-named girls (you know, the ones whose mothers gave them their maiden name as a middle name? It was super common at St. Paul's). She came from a small, predominantly black town in the Deep South. My guess was she had never really interacted with the black people in her hometown on account of the fact that her family basically ran the place. Who knows. I never took the time to get to know her and her origin story after that run-in. But, even though I now despised Hannah, I found most of the other white girls on campus to be fairly decent people.

I loved hanging out with the black boys in Nash House. The black and brown dudes liked to live in huge mobs in either Nash or Wing. A group of ten friends would agree to all select the same dorm on their housing form. The result was a beautiful thing: a mix of

African-, Caribbean-, South Asian—, and Korean-inflected hip hop culture that completely transformed the climate of those residential spaces. They were all in different rooms, but it felt like one big room because everyone was so connected, like one united community. You could walk into Nash and completely forget you were at the epicenter of New England preppydom. They would bump Wu-Tang Clan mad loud. The bass pulsated through the walls. I would walk into the building and hear:

Cash rules everything around me.
C.R.E.A.M.
get the money
Dolla, Dolla bill y'all

It was like they were daring one of the square white boys to ask them to turn it down.

In their space, I felt like I could just be my black tomboy self, running from room to room in my baggy jeans and oversize checkered flannels. I could use all the so-called ebonics that I was used to back home but was now discouraged from using at St. Paul's, letting "I'm finna" and "they be doin'" and "I been tryna tell you" fly like I used to back in the rowdy cafeteria of Village Woods Middle School. The black boys were *allowed* to be loud and bombastic. Their version of black cool was accepted. They could be hip hop with their baggy jeans and wheat Timberland boots and cornrows, like my cousin Jonathan used to wear, and still be thought of as smart and athletic. In fact, that year, one of the black guys who lived in Wing, a sixth former from Brooklyn, was president of the entire student body. That was huge.

For black girls and Latinas, there was more social pressure for us to conform, to tame our hair and our bodies. In order to cope, the girls would find a bestie who became the center of their social world, and they would form a bond that typically lasted their entire four years at St. Paul's. The pair would room together but not in big crews like the boys, often sacrificing their shot at living in the nicest dorms in order to ensure that they could stay together. So when I visited girl students, auditioning potential besties, I'd often have to travel to four different dorms just to see folks. It was something of a hassle, but I wasn't doing much studying in those early days anyway. Plus, I quickly found that I needed the support and wisdom from the older girls, girls who could relate to my hairstyling woes and issues back home—girls like Nikki from Chicago, whose room always smelled like warm vanilla thanks to her scented oil diffuser. You could walk into the older girls' rooms and feel like you had been transported into a sanctuary. The girls kept their music relatively low, but you betta believe they too were always playing some hip hop and R&B. I think it was Nikki who introduced me to the Fugees' infectious "Nappy Heads" and Da Youngsta's' groove "Hip Hop Ride."

My St. Paul's bestie ended up being a café au lait–complexioned black girl in my form from Brooklyn named Shandrica. I always thought she was part Latina because she lived in Simpson near three older Latinas from New York. Plus, to my ears, she sounded like Rosie Perez in *Do the Right Thing* and was always talking about Dominican hair salons. (But I would discover, after we had been friends for decades, that she was in fact not Afro-Latina!) I noticed her instantly because, like me, she rolled up to campus in braids, the *blackest* black girl braids I'd ever seen. They were medium-size cornrows that

started behind her right ear and circled around her head like a bee-
hive, with some of the rows sweeping across her forehead like a bang,
reconnecting on the other side of her head, and then falling into a
cascade of braids that stopped in front of her right ear. It was a full 360
of cornrows! She later jokingly referred to the style as "the swim cap."
Apparently, some St. Paul's kids had teased her about those braids,
giving them that nickname on account of how the braids squeezed her
entire forehead tight like a swim cap. They were definitely a conversation piece, but she got mad compliments on them in Brooklyn,
with folks stopping her on the street to ask for her braider's phone
number. Shandrica had on a pair of red baggy jeans, some sneakers, and
a white long-sleeved, oversize Malcolm X t-shirt. I peeped her style,
thinking she was a black girl's black girl. But also like a black girl,
she wasn't quick to become all bubbly and open. She was reserved,
like me, taking in the scene before she committed to liking a thing.

I can't even remember when or how we clicked. But a rapper
definitely had something to do with it. Shandrica's room in Simpson
was relatively unadorned, but she had a huge poster of the finest
man I had ever seen over her bed. He had the smoothest honey-
brown skin and perfect lips that served as a sensual counterbalance
to his serious chocolate-brown eyes. Those eyes pierced my soul,
and I was in love . . . with a poster. "Who's Nas?" (pronouncing
Nas with a short *a* sound like *apple*) I asked giddily, butterflies having traveled up from the pit of my stomach and now were flittering
all over my vocal chords. "It's Nahhhs," Shandrica said, kinda snarky
but kinda relating to my awe. "Short for Nasir. Nasir Jones." Deeper
in love I fell. Instantly. His name was so black, so *conscious*. I hadn't
heard him rap one bar, but I already knew he was a beast on the mic.
He was my boyfriend. In my head, at least. (One day, ten years later,

I sat across from the man on the poster in a restaurant in New York City. All of my fifteen-year-old feelings rushed to the surface. Of course, this was before I heard his ex-wife Kelis's allegations that he used to beat her.)

The World Wide Web wasn't yet a thing, so it wasn't like I could internet stalk this Nas. The only way I could be close to him was to visit Shandrica and peer at his poster while his raspy voice perfectly narrated ghetto tales, rolling over beats made by now legendary hip hop producers Large Professor, Pete Rock, and DJ Premier. And over our Nas *Illmatic* soundtrack, Shan, as I had taken to calling her, and I exchanged stories about our families, hobbies, and secret crushes. By winter break, we were making plans to be roommates next school year. I had found my person, my secret keeper, my other half. Sixth months apart in age, we were cut from the same Cross Colours cloth in many ways, but still different enough that we could also occupy our own social spaces at St. Paul's. I understood now the bestie coupling thing. You needed a safe space to just *be*—not being loud like with the black guys, and not doing the preppy performance with the white kids.

I was finding my way in my new world. I'd adapted to the preppy lingo like "vis-dis" for visual design and "fro-yo" for the frozen yogurt treats we used to have delivered from a spot in town, and the preppy nerd slang like "horrendous" and "horrific," which we said ad nauseam in the way hood kids said "yo" and "dope" and "fresh." I balanced out my collection of baggy jeans with modest dresses. I was even considering asking Mom or Dad to buy me a pair of silk J. Crew long johns because Juli said they were super comfortable and practical for both winter and summer wear (a purchase that would've solidified my buppydom).

My grades were improving; I was taking advantage of this Chaucer- and Shakespeare-heavy education, enjoying our science excursions, and making plans to study abroad. I was taking SAT prep courses and considering attending one of the Ivies or the Seven Sisters schools for college. Previously the most ambitious options on my radar were the Big Ten schools and perhaps Notre Dame. I had joined the gospel choir and was taking classical voice lessons. And I was making friends, even with the white kids; they had stopped being one monolithic blob of privilege to me. Now I was listening to Hole and the Cranberries, finding space in my sonic landscape for "Doll Parts" and "Zombie," as I bonded with Ella, the bohemian from upstate New York, and her roommate, Tess, the black girl from Wisconsin who I used to think of as an Oreo but now adored. I never loved this music in the same way I loved hip hop, but I was learning that it had its own way of soothing me.

When I flew home that spring, I cried the entire plane ride. Eyes red-rimmed, I peered out the Northwest Airlines plane window. I wouldn't return to St. Paul's the following school year. You see, those baggy jeans were concealing a secret: I was four months pregnant. I would return home to have my baby and graduate from a local high school. And it was as if the puffs of smoke from Fort Wayne's many factories knew I wouldn't be going back to my East Coast life. They dotted the sky, instructing my plane on where to land, where to return the girl who thought she had escaped the town's grasp.

6

Coochie Cutters

My cloudy eyes slowly blinked open. A sliver of light filtered through the cheap plaid curtains that framed the window. I panned the room, lined with 70s-era furnishings. In the bed next to mine was a tangle of caramel-colored limbs. My eyes focused and found the faces of the couple the limbs belonged to: it was Crystal and David, my *new* old friends—the couple I'd met in real life only the day before. I was too far away from the ocean to smell a sea breeze, but at least now I remembered where I was. I had fled Indiana for Atlanta before hopping a Greyhound bus and riding nearly four hundred miles east to Myrtle Beach, South Carolina, to meet some friends I'd been chatting with online.

Just a day earlier, I'd shoved several pairs of Wal-Mart short shorts, which we called "coochie cutters," some matching tank tops, a handful of frilly panties that screamed "I'm an adult!," a matronly looking bathing suit, and a random selection of shoes into my mom's old Calvin Klein suitcase. I headed from posh Dunwoody—a neighborhood just on the outside of Atlanta's 285 loop—to the Forsyth Street bus station downtown. It was the hastiest, most dangerous thing I'd done in my life up to that point. But I was grown, right? I'd just graduated from high school in Indiana and was looking to set out on my own journey, willing to take any mode of transportation required to get to the real life that I imagined waited for me in the South.

I was searching for a sense of freedom that life post–high school promised, but what I found was that coochie cutters were a metaphor for life as a late teen searching for adulthood: sexy looking but a bit uncomfortable. *Coochie* was among other words like *twat*, *split*, *cut*, and *pussy* that we peppered our language with when mentioning the vagina. And *cutters* can mean two different things, depending on whether you're inside or outside of the shorts. For me, it vividly conjures up the discomfort of wearing shorts that are so tight and short in the crotch that they can *cut* circulation, putting your coochie to sleep. But *cutters* can also refer to the fact that the shorts showcase the "cut" or split of the vagina, a silhouette that some find sexy. Other names for these shorts popular across the Caribbean communicate a similar idea: pum-pum shorts, batty riders, bum riders, chocha shorts. The shorts clung to every crevice.

Atlanta-based rapper Playa Poncho released "Koochie Kuterz" in 1995, a fast-paced, 808-bumping club banger that reverenced the short shorts and solidified its colloquial name: *"Look at dem girls, they kickin' dem koochie kuterz"* the chorus went. Here I was packing off to Myrtle Beach in the late 90s in my ill-fitting coochie cutters in a quest to be grown and independent and carefree. I had no qualms about crushing my vulva for endless hours on a bus or putting myself in all sorts of stranger danger as I attempted to find the real me.

I blame AOL for this little excursion of mine. See, a little over a year earlier, the internet portal and online community started sending these free trial discs to my mother's house. Mom wasn't tech-savvy. Neither was I, really. And the World Wide Web was this obscure virtual space that few everyday folks understood. I'd been throwing the discs away without even opening them. But then I spent some time at my dad's house, which was wired with AOL, and I realized its potential to give me an out from the suffocating discomfort of Fort Wayne. My feelings about being here had become more complex, but no happier in the two years since I'd returned from boarding school.

So when I saw the billionth disc in the mail, I decided to open this one up: a thin sleeve that held a CD with the iconic AOL pyramid and all-seeing eye with the words "One Month Free!" printed in a bold color. I recalled the fun I had dialing up at Dad's and roaming through chat rooms under his username. I convinced Mom that we needed AOL ASAP. She didn't know anything about this technology, but she applied the same mentality to tech as she did to fashion: she wanted the thing that was new and cutting edge, the thing that folks in our neighborhood hadn't been *put on* to yet. And AOL was it. I walked her through the steps to initiate her account and create an AOL email address (which she still has today). It would be the first time of many that I hooked us up: the thirty-day trial discs kept coming, and I kept using them up. All told, we had AOL for nearly a year without ever paying member fees.

Those monthly discs that showed up in our mailbox, right there with the credit card sign-ups and other junk mail, connected a black girl from Indiana to people around the world. I needed this.

I was rummaging through a drawer one day and came across those old lime-green Boss jeans that I wore constantly when I was away at St. Paul's School. I remembered how they hid my pregnancy so well. The colorful baggy jeans trend was now over, and just like an old fashion trend, I had tucked away my St. Paul's life in a drawer, embarrassed and ashamed that I had participated in the first place.

In Fort Wayne, I didn't have to hide my pregnancy. "Babies having babies," as the church folk called it, was no new phenomenon in my hometown. Plus, I didn't get big enough to show until the last week or so of my pregnancy, so I never really needed maternity clothes. I wore the same leggings and tunics and short shorts as the rest of the girls in my classes, blending in on the outside while feeling emotionally wrenched on the inside.

My baby boy—Malik, I named him—was almost two, and we were cobbling out some sort of life together under my mother's roof. I tried hard not to think about what I'd sacrificed when I'd decided to keep him (or what my mother had sacrificed), but the sight of those lime-green jeans pulled so many complicated emotions to the fore.

I was a different person after my boarding school experience; worldly, they call it. Once you've seen the world, or at least a rich, WASPy slice of it, you can't go back, your soul craves the adventures of the unknown. The discount store Dickies and flannels and hoodies that were just part of the normal background when I went away now seemed like garments that actively stifled my creativity. They wanted to smother my worldliness; the deep sense of self and community belonging that they used to hold wasn't there anymore. It was clear: I had become haughty in my time away, not an Oreo, but definitely some brand of bougie black girl. I had turned my back on Fort Wayne. Now having barely reformulated myself, I was "home," and neither of us was ready.

But Fort Wayne had turned its back on *me* first, I rationalized. It had been telling me since I was a little girl that I was a defective cog in our factory town machine. That by wanting *more* or *different* I was somehow the problem. If only I had been willing to just accept the course of life that Fort Wayne had to offer. But I hadn't been then, and I definitely wasn't now. Not now that I knew that my boarding school friends were learning in a week what it took my teachers a whole marking period to present and doing study abroad trips to small villages in Mexico with names like Tepoztlán and vacationing with their families in the South of France. These were the folks I'd be competing with for coveted slots in private East Coast colleges and then for dream jobs—if I could ever break away from Fort Wayne again.

AOL quickly became my daily escape from the constant, unrelenting pain of being rejected by both worlds and the demands of young motherhood. My life online mattered more than my IRL social life. In the real world (which felt like the fake one to me at the time), I was reluctantly making friends in a new school district, now in high school with kids I hadn't laid eyes on since second grade. I wasn't in on the longstanding friendships that the black kids had solidified in middle school (when I was with my friends over at

Village Woods, in the other district). I've always been a social person, so I became vice president of my class and a varsity cheerleader, and I made good friends eventually. But even so I felt empty. Disconnected. I basically dialed in my entire senior year, there but not really present. There was a part of my life experience that I couldn't share, couldn't even explain to these new friends. With AOL, I could find friends with experiences like mine, people who didn't know about my "baggage."

I would speed home in my mom's silver Mitsubishi Mirage, which had essentially become my car since she drove her squad car everywhere, and throw my book bag down and dial up the AOL gods. In the days before avatars, your username, color, and font were your calling card. HazelEyes1998 was my moniker, styled in pink Comic Sans or Lucida Calligraphy font. I lived in the chat rooms, gravitating toward the black life–oriented rooms. My chatting felt wild and carefree. I jumped into the fray, immediately able to see that people had complex, long-term relationships and identities in this chat world. I learned the lingo and rules—oftentimes by pissing someone off first—@ mentioning people to talk to them directly, learning how to draw what we now call emojis [:o)], and hearts [<3 < 3 <3], and flowers [@—>—-] with the punctuation keys. It was all so techy and new. Everything evolved rapidly as people in the chat community debated music, movies, and TV shows; shared dating woes; traded sex stories; cracked jokes on one another; and debated which sororities and fraternities were better. After forming quick bonds with people in the big chat rooms, I would send them each a buddy request. As buddies we could see when the other was online, send instant messages, and create private chat threads.

In those days, we were being inundated with messages about the dangers of the World Wide Web. And I was sure that those dangers lurked out there. I mean, there was a possibility that none of these people were who they said they were. But my attitude was some mix of midwestern girl naiveté, the (false) belief that black folks didn't play such games, and a simple lack of caring. I returned to the chat rooms every day, becoming something of a promiscuous social butterfly, sometimes juggling two chat rooms and five or six private chats at the same time, while doing homework, fixing dinner for Malik, and tying up my mother's phone line for hours.

I also used AOL as a virtual college tour. There were chat rooms specifically for folks who attended historically black colleges and universities, HBCUs, and I would chat up these folks to get a feel for their campus cultures. This much I had figured out: I needed to get away from Fort Wayne, and I needed to flee the white culture that seemed to cast a long shadow over black life in the city. I wanted to attend a black college in the South. I wanted to get to the blackest part of the country possible. The top choices: Howard University in Washington, DC, the "chocolate city"; Clark Atlanta University in "Hotlanta," the black mecca; and Hampton University in bougie Hampton, Virginia. At these places, I could find the black self that I had never encountered, especially not at St. Paul's. I just needed to find my people. I pursued black colleges with a militancy that made my super black dashiki mother proud.

In early 1998, I was accepted to all of the HBCUs I'd applied to. There was never a question in my parents' mind that I'd go to college somewhere. They would help: Dad would pay and Mom would keep Malik until I got settled. I decided to attend Clark Atlanta. Atlanta was where I needed to be, honey! The city had a huge constellation of schools, including the four HBCUs in the Atlanta University

Center: Clark Atlanta, Spelman College, Morehouse College, and Morris Brown College. Atlanta was the home of some of my favorite hip hop and R&B artists: Outkast, Goodie Mob, Xscape, Da Brat, Kris Kross, Raheem the Dream, K. P. & Envyi, TLC, Usher, and Lil Jon & The East Side Boyz. They were changing the game with their stomp-worthy breakbeats and seductive harmonies. Atlanta was the undisputed epicenter of black culture.

Plus, it helped that Mom's good friend Loretta and her kids had resettled in Atlanta. Mom and I had visited them a few times when I was in elementary school, so I had met the city, and I'd made chat friends already who were also planning to head there to one of the HBCUs. I devoted my energy during the spring of my senior year to making friends with the people who would be central, as I envisioned it, to my new life in Atlanta.

One day in an HBCU chat room, I met a girl named CAUPanther02. We began chatting and I learned that her name was Crystal, she was from Greenville, South Carolina, and she would be an incoming freshman at Clark Atlanta in the fall. Crystal seemed ambitious like me, and, like me, she had a plush kindness that us small-town girls are taught to exude. We were internet besties. I would talk to her about the latest drama in my high school and she about hers. We exchanged some grainy photos over AOL, which seemed way high-tech at the time, and eventually we talked on the phone too. We planned on being suitemates in Beckwith Hall, one of Clark Atlanta's freshman dorms. She had a boyfriend named David, also from South Carolina, who was currently a freshman at Morehouse. I think their relationship started online too; at this point they were in a committed LDR (long-distance relationship). I became friends with David too, and the three of us would create our own private chats—me from my den in Fort Wayne, Crystal from her living room in Greenville, and David from his dorm room in Atlanta. David was the sage who schooled us about college life, and he connected me with girls who were upperclassmen at Clark Atlanta. By the time my high school graduation rolled around, my aspirational new world was taking shape, and Crystal and David were a major part of it.

Crystal and I kept plotting and planning a time when we could meet each other IRL, and the opportunity quickly presented itself when all the pieces came together for me to move to Atlanta early. Mom agreed that I could head there and live with Loretta in her luxury Dunwoody apartment. "Yes! Go 'head, go 'head!!" I yelled out loud and started doing the cabbage patch, my celebration dance, when Mom shared her decision with me. In exchange, though, I would help Loretta launch her catering business (she was tired of being a cop). It worked for me. Loretta had already raised two kids to adulthood and had no interest in playing my adopted mother. She treated me like a young professional and allowed me to coordinate my own social life. So, from Loretta's desktop, I connected with Crystal and David and planned our trip to Myrtle Beach, the working man's paradise sitting on a sixty-mile strip of Carolina coastline called the Grand Strand. In pictures, Myrtle Beach looked so luxurious to my landlocked eyes; it could've been the French Riviera. My only prior encounter with a beach consisted of the brief minutes I'd spent at Venice Beach with my aunt Brenda when I was a kid—and those moments were pretty glamorous in my memory. I was ready to ball on a budget in Myrtle Beach with my new friends. Loretta helped me check the Greyhound timetable and drove me to the bus station, but I kept my mom in the dark about my trip. This was me, grown Tanisha, making her own decisions.

I honestly didn't give much thought to what I was tossing in the suitcase as I packed up my coochie cutters in all of their sexy and fun and adventurous and mostly practical glory. I had never gone on a girls' trip and didn't know that such trips are a quiet competition, all about looking as cute, if not cuter, than the girls you're with in order to rep the crew right *in them streets*, so my sense of the stakes was unrealistically low. Short shorts definitely can be cute, of course. Women have been wearing them since the early twentieth century—especially women of African descent who live in areas where they suit the warm climate—and making them stylish for just as long. Short shorts hit the global market in the 1970s, when French ready-to-wear lines put them on the runway in high-end fabrics like satin and velvet. Leading fashion publication *Women's Wear Daily* dubbed the barely there bottoms "hot pants," and that name has stuck with the industry version of the garment. To let my mom's baby sister, Marcia, tell it, my mother had fully bought into the hot-pants craze as a teen in Cleveland: "Oh, she would strut around in her hot pants and a long vest, with her false eyelashes and her French roll, thinking she belonged on the pages of *Vogue*!" My shorts had exactly as much glam as Wal-Mart had on offer.

I also didn't consider how uncomfortable it would be to travel for twelve hours on a thrumming, jolting, minimally cushioned public bus in coochie cutters. It felt like we stopped in every small Southern town possible between Atlanta and Myrtle Beach. My thighs, exposed in my tight denim shorts, stuck to the vinyl bus seat as I struggled to settle into the ambient temperature and not become nauseated by the random smells. I hadn't ridden a Greyhound since I was a kid. This will be an adventure, I convinced myself. The trip itself was no big deal. Mom and me had racked up nearly twenty magnets representing all the states we'd traveled to together, mostly by car, so I was comfortable traveling. I'd have to grab a South Carolina magnet for the collection.

I wasn't concerned about the obvious things—like what would happen if Crystal and David, who had booked our hotel room, never showed up. Cell phone technology wasn't yet a thing among everyday folk, so there was no way to follow up to verify times. All I had was my clear Motorola beeper that Mom was about to stop paying for. Where would I go if they stood me up? What if they were there, but turned out to be very different from the people I expected? What if they raped and killed me? Nothing of this nature even really occurred to me. I had a lot of faith that these eighteen- and nineteen-year-olds were gonna be there for me. And be sane.

The bus at long last teetered into the tiny Myrtle Beach bus station. And I, seated in the back in typical teenager style, waited for the passengers to file out before I sauntered off the bus, heart beating rapidly and excitedly as I prepared to meet my AOL buddies. I stepped down the awkwardly spaced bus steps and out into the blazing hot sea air. I scanned the parking lot, trying not to be super obvious that I was looking for someone, slightly anxious now.

A loud "Tanisha!" told me I'd been spotted. I'm glad Crystal could find me based on my picture, because I would not have been able to recognize her from hers. Crystal's little AOL photos hadn't done her justice. She was *gorgeous*. Slightly shorter than me, she was a pretty shade of honey brown, with a Halle Berry–type haircut: short layers on top, with blond and light brown high- and lowlights, that perfectly blended into tapered sides and back. I had been wearing short haircuts since middle school, but Crystal's cut was so precise and easy in the way her relaxed curls blended into the taper. Her eyes

were a soft amber brown, accentuated by just the slightest dark cir-
cles around her puffy eyelids that gave them the same raccoon halo as
mine. She was wearing a tank top that hugged her small breasts,
she had a tiny waist that formed into round hips and perfectly shaped,
thick honey thighs and calves that peeked out from under her short
skirt. Crystal sported a pair of navy blue Candies and her toes were
cute and tiny and freshly painted. David was over six feet tall, and
my shade of reddish brown. He had described himself as looking like
one of the Wayans brothers, and yeah, I could see that. Like a blend
of Marlon and Damon Wayans, with squinty eyes, a keen nose,
and a wide, straight smile covered in a track of braces that were about
ready to be removed. He had on a button-down linen shirt that was
open, showing his bare, lean-yet-toned chest and abs, and long
board shorts and deck shoes. Crystal and David looked easy and
carefree, like they had just finished bonin' and were still adorned in
the afterglow.

I felt unprepared. Insecure. I was out of place with this young,
effortlessly sexy couple. It was that feeling when you realize that
you have *grossly* misjudged a thing you've been looking forward to.
The way Crystal had explained herself online always made her sound
like a bookish, slightly socially awkward girl, a girl like me. One that
didn't put much effort into her looks. Maybe she really didn't, but
if that's how she saw herself, she had one distorted view. She was a
goddess, curvy and thick in all of the ways the boys I grew up with
in Indiana loved. I myself was a recent initiate in the thickums club,
sporting a new Depo-Provera-enhanced booty and thick muscular
thighs developed by track-and-field, cheerleading, and dance practices. Still, I felt the sting of the many years of being teased for being too thin: limby legs and lanky arms, a flat chest and no butt or

hips to speak of. Black folks in Fort Wayne loved size—perhaps it's our southern roots—and, to them, I always looked like I needed a meal. Then I had a baby, got on Depo, gained twenty pounds, and started to get compliments. The boys were finally seeing me as sexy and grown: "Damn! Tanisha had a baby and got thick!"

But even with my new meat, I didn't stack up like Crystal because, as the hip hop music videos were starting to teach us, it wasn't just about *size*, it was about *shape*. Crystal had curves, no matter which direction you looked at her from. Her butt was a perfect heart shape and her thighs had a lot of meat on the quads, with the perfect amount of jiggle. Her knees hyperextended, which made her thighs look plumper and showcased her meaty calves. She'd be plus-size by garment-industry-modeling standards, but she was absolutely perfect by urban modeling specs. If she lived in Fort Wayne, she would have easily been one of the sexiest girls in my high school. Naturally slim David had to be rejoicing in all those curves.

When model and popular *Jet* magazine fashion correspondent Audrey Smaltz renamed hot pants "knockout shorts" in the 1970s on account of the fact that black women wore them because they accentuated their knockout bodies, she had a body like Crystal's in mind; she was definitely *Jet* "Beauty of the Week" material. Smaltz wanted to come up with a competing term as an acknowledgment that our black body norms aren't the same as the white high-fashion industry's, and change the way you see the garment's appeal. A fashion feels different when it's a different fit that's idolized, and in the black community, meatiness was ideal. Knockout shorts were shorts that flattered *our* notion of a killer body.

Alas, I, tall and straight up and down plus a little new mass, even in my short shorts, didn't feel sexually free. I mean, clearly I wasn't a virgin, but I wasn't experiencing the freedom or confidence that I wanted to come along with sex. I was always in pursuit of feminine girliness, never quite finding it or feeling like I measured up, and having sex just made me feel more insecure about how I stacked up to the women on TV and in movies. It's this thing that folks call teen angst. That uneasiness that was exacerbated when we tried to do grown folks' things. I didn't consider myself noticeably pretty. Perhaps cute, on account of my baby face that made me look younger than my years. And then I had a maturity about me that read older age-wise. But that didn't translate into sexiness and it definitely did not translate into fine, the definitive superlative to me, the ultimate combination of being jaw-droppingly gorgeous *and* extremely sexy.

So I was intimidated by Crystal. But looking back at a picture of us next to each other on that first meeting in the parking lot, in hindsight, I can acknowledge that we actually were a striking pair. Where Crystal was curvy and feminine in all the right ways, I was at least three inches taller, in peak athletic form with long wet-and-wavy microbraids. The Atlanta sun had turned my skin a coppery reddish brown that made me look luminous. And I had painted my nails a soft coral pink, which was a nice contrast to the black shellac-y polish on Crystal's long-clawed acrylic nails and toes. We were like night and day. And David seemed to find the contrast intoxicating. I imagined I could see the wheels of his brain turning, maybe plotting ways to convince Crystal and me to have one of those ménage à trois I assumed he and his horny college friends were always fantasizing about.

I couldn't stop staring at Crystal as we walked to the car. I studied her every move with both envy and awe, watching her butt jiggle as the wooden soles of her Candies struck the concrete. I can't remember the make and model of the car they were driving, but if I wanted to capture this young couple's effortless, beachy vintage glamour, a red 1970 Mustang convertible is the only car that could truly fit the picture.

We drove several blocks to our hotel, making awkward conversation in the car, trying to come to grips with the fact that we were now all of a sudden in each other's physical space. David, the more outgoing of the two, filled in a lot of the dead air, letting his shy girlfriend retreat to the fringes of the conversation. I was a bit disappointed that Crystal didn't seem to be very present in the moment, but I soon learned that that was just her way. She had a moody disposition. Really, the reason I could relate to Crystal was because she was an artist who hadn't yet figured out how to tap into her artistic side, because everyone, David included, had her trapped in her sexy, thick-girl image. I connected with the deeper, brooding energy that festered within her. For now, her soul was an unknown quantity, hidden beneath the face and body of video vixen Melyssa Ford.

We made it back to our shabby hotel, and I unpacked my belongings as Crystal and David disappeared into the shower together. I was now questioning everything that I had haphazardly tossed in my luggage. There wasn't much diversity in the outfits I'd brought. Everything was hot pants. But here's the thing: if the pants are so named because the length is like a barometer, barely covering the genitals being a hundred degrees, then my hot pants were room temperature, at best. For some, true hot pants have to bare the bottom of the butt cheeks (for others, this is precisely why the style is lewd and vulgar), and mine were more like mid-thigh. It all changes from body to body though. The thicker and curvier the wearer's body is, the shorter the shorts appear. When I was in middle school, the few white girls in my classes were wearing those shorts and the admin-istration did not see them as too short or revealing or sexy, but on a black girl's frame, particularly a thick black girl with a booty and thighs, the shorts were instantly sexualized. That girl's body con-sidered excessive and too much for school: I saw so many girls sent home for wearing them. With my figure, though, in terms of my grown and sexy goals on this trip, my shorts were just too long.

We were young but wanted to be so grown. I was always trying to channel my mother, which meant that I kept aiming for polished young professional and hitting matronly. At the time, I consid-ered myself fashion-forward, but wasn't really, not in the ways that I'd come to experience fashion in the South. Since I had been back in Fort Wayne, with its limited shopping options, I had taken to shopping at some of the old spots that had filled my closet in my pre–boarding school days, which meant that most of my hot pants came from discount stores, including Wal-Mart, which had quickly become my mom's favorite haunt. At the time, I was not opposed to Wal-Mart clothes either. I could take some of their basic sepa-rates and jazz them up into looks that felt stylish. My motel room drawer now displayed the results of my foray into discount fashion: some leather belts and four pairs of coochie cutters, in khaki, blue jean, cream denim, and one in a dusty-pink khaki material. I'd brought a few cheap tank tops, one long-sleeved white collared shirt that I could wear over my tanks if it got chilly at night, a lime-green tankini, and a black-and-white polka dot one-piece that looked like the vintage swimdresses women wore in the 1950s.

And sunglasses. Mine weren't some fancy brand, but they were on trend: a pair of big-face, round, black sunglasses that rappers Lil' Kim and Foxy Brown had helped make popular. Traditionally, I never liked to wear sunglasses because people told me my light eyes were pretty, so why cover them? But I had this new move that I thought seemed grown and seductive. I would wear sunglasses and then occasionally remove the glasses in a slow, tantalizing manner to reveal my greenish-brown eyes for the benefit of a fine guy passing by. I'm sure it looked more *thirsty* than alluring more often than not.

I had bought a pair of chunky-heeled sandals from Bakers, my favorite shoe store at the time on account that they made knockoff versions of the latest high-end styles at affordable mall prices. They were amber brown, with two brown plastic chain links that connected the thick band over the toe to the ankle strap. They were the baddest things coming. I also had a pair of burnt orange Candies with a wooden sole. I had planned to alternate these dressier shoes with a pair of flip-flops and some Wal-Mart-brand Birkenstocks, so that I could dress my hot pants up or down. But now, all of these purchases seemed momish and uncool.

This trip to Myrtle Beach was where I really noticed just how conservative my look was. In terms of the staunch Christian standards that prevailed back home, I was a "loose" girl because of my liberal dashiki upbringing. Mom wasn't invested in tropes of *good* girl and *bad* girl that rested upon how a woman dressed and what that said about her morals or her sexual availability. Mom never lectured me about such things. In fact, she let me navigate much of that on my own, and it was something that the older girls she mentored and helped raise always loved about her. But she raised me with a fairly modest sense of style for her own reasons.

Mom's own sagacity when it came to clothes and sexiness was more on the athletic side. She wore hot pants, but the *way* she wore them said a lot about the aesthetic that I ended up copying from her. I can remember a family trip to King's Island for my eighth birthday and Mom wearing some black jersey-knit hot pants that barely covered her butt and showcased her long, toned legs. She rocked a spaghetti-strap black tank, navy Adidas Samoas, and a straw fedora, cocked to the side, over a camouflage bandanna covering her hair. It was athleisure wear before athleisure wear was a thing. She was indeed sexy with her legs out, but the sporty feel of the outfit rooted her sexy in something that was not conventionally feminine. This type of sexuality, Mom thought, was smarter, more complex, more intriguing and alluring than simply baring everything. She never really said it or put other women down for their choices, but I picked up on her attitude: Make your pretty and your sexy interesting. Lead with a sense of confidence.

And that was all great. In theory. But as I looked at Crystal as she sauntered out of the steamy bathroom in spandex, I felt even more self-conscious about the odd-length shorts on my sporty body. Crystal was wearing a pair of taupe ponte pants that, if I'd looked at the label, likely would have read "Express" and a leopard-print spaghetti tank with a peplum that opened in the front and showed off her creamy abdomen. Express was the epitome of mall couture back then. It was the gateway store for teens looking to move into the adult styles we'd seen our older sisters and cousins wear. The price points were inflated for the quality, but Express had all of the cool silhouettes, including their signature ponte pants in every color, and they were carrying the latest flashy costume jewelry. Mom wasn't shelling out for Express in those days, so I had to be content with window wishing at the Express store in the white mall,

Glenbrook, on the north side, and then going to Wal-Mart, Value City, TJ Maxx, Deb, and other discount stores to try to replicate the looks. The white girls at my high school shopped at Express, the Buckle, and the Limited. Those stores were a big deal for them. They wanted outfits that you could recognize as off the rack from these stores. In Mom's opinion, those white girl stores were too commercial and manufactured. She preferred to cobble things together from high-end stores like L. S. Ayres, her vintage boutiques, the Goodwill, and rummage sales. But Crystal was doing something more interesting with these standard-issue mall clothes than the frail white girls I grew up with. She was channeling an energy similar to Lisa Nicole Carson's thick and sultry character, Marti, in *Jason's Lyric*: a brand of black country girl couture flavored by savory shrimp-n-grits and ham hocks and black-eyed peas.

After my own shower I emerged in a salmon pink "body shirt," as we called it, a spandex shirt that hugged my body, and my khaki hot pants. It was the sexiest thing I'd packed. I was Jackie Joyner-Kersee to Crystal's Lisa Nicole. I put on my Bakers sandals to try to dress the thing up a bit, make it look more adult. But it was just this super-odd look that made no sense. The khaki shorts and the cinnamon-brown braided belt read summer camp counselor, and my pink shirt, that had too much sateen sheen to be really fashion-forward (I mean, on other occasions I'd paired it with a floral-printed skirt for school functions), and my Bakers sandals looked like I was auditioning for the role of "Smart College Girl #2" in R&B group Shai's "Baby I'm Yours" music video. I stared at myself in the mirror, trying to push past this rush of insecurity. I freed my braids from the hair tie that I had carelessly wrapped around them as I showered and tossed the back-length braids over one shoulder, framing my makeup-free face. I had found me. Again. I was ready to hit the streets. I wished I looked a bit sexier but you still couldn't tell me nothing.

A sea of black teens flooded Ocean Boulevard. It was Senior Week, a famed holiday for graduating high school seniors in South Carolina. They all pack up and head to Myrtle Beach for unbridled teenage fun: drinking, hook-ups, and rabble-rousing. It felt like a Hype Williams music video—everything was slow-motion cool, colors bright and highly saturated, black skin poppin'! Black folks were hanging off the balconies of hotels with beach-themed names like Windsurfer, Sea Gypsy Inn, Yachtsman. Cars with boomin' Alpine and Kenwood sound systems careened through the streets. Dudes on motorcycles carried girls with short skirts that rode up, exposing their bikini bottoms. I had never seen this audacious a display of black revelry. These teenagers had transformed the whole space in a way my factory town peers would never have dreamed of. At most after our graduation we might have gone to Cedar Point amusement park in Sandusky, Ohio, for the day. In all honesty, we were never raised to believe that we could coordinate something as big as a multiday trip like this on our own.

All of the girls in Myrtle Beach got the coochie cutters memo. Girls were strutting in their short shorts, with sneakers, heels, or those on-trend Candies. Some in tanks, halters, and tube tops, others in jerseys, baby tees, and fitted Polo shirts. All of my insecurities about my lack of sexy dissipated as I reveled in the range of hot-pants-fueled self-expression in the streets. I couldn't have articulated it at the time, but I was wearing a garment that connected me to black women around the world through a shared cultural language. Songs by dancehall queen Patra, who had some commercial success in the

U.S. with "Worker Man" and "Romantic Call" (featuring West Coast rapper Yo-Yo) had introduced us Indiana girls to the phrase *pum-pum shorts*. There is something about booty shorts that makes them instantly recognizable across the diaspora as youthful and irreverent. My friends and I were into them because the shorts were all over the hip hop videos that played on repeat on BET and MTV. Parents would worry that the shorts made their daughters look too "fast," but they'd often write it off, saying it's best to wear shorts like that when you're young and stacked and built like a brick house.

"Look at them girls with them Dazzey Duks on" was pulsing in our ears that year, thanks to Miami bass duo Duice's infectious track that made you want to twerk and pump whenever it came on. It came out when I was in middle school, but for some reason folks had rediscovered it. That damn song was everywhere! Daisy Duke was from the TV show *The Dukes of Hazzard*, which aired from 1979 to 1985. Daisy, in her iconic short shorts, was a mainstay on my television in elementary school. "Dazzey Duks" reimagined Daisy as a black woman, Dazzey, re-rooting the shorts in the (global) black southern traditions of music and dance and style.

To the eyes of one half of the culture, all that deep Miami bass was meant to get girls to dance and pump and twerk with their short shorts on for the pleasure of men. But that's not why we picked these garments off the rack or cut them out of an old pair of jeans. We were mostly wearing them for ourselves. It was a rite of passage of sorts to wear your booty shorts to a picnic, trip to the amusement park, or school talent show. We would cut them really short and wash them to make them fringe at the bottom and then wear spandex biker shorts in wild colors or patterns underneath. Or we would use puffy paints and a hot-glue gun to bedazzle them with rhinestones.

Or we'd take them to the mall to get our nicknames airbrushed across the butt.

Now, I was sharing this rite of passage with a sea of other members of the class of 1998, black high school graduates poised to take over the world. In my haste to exit Fort Wayne, I had sped through homecoming and prom and graduation. Graduating from high school was so expected for me that I hadn't even taken a pause to reflect on the fact that it was an accomplishment, one that several in my family had never achieved, one that my grandparents had fled Alabama for me to be able to attain. When I agreed to come to Myrtle Beach, I had no clue that Senior Week was a thing, but I quickly became a member of the Myrtle Beach student council and made up for all the celebration I'd skipped in my senior year back in Fort Wayne.

We strolled around that night as music blared and underage folks imbibed secret stashes of Tanqueray and Absolut. I wasn't a drinker. But the energy of it was intoxicating. We passed Ripley's Believe It or Not! and ran through the Nightmare Haunted House, a narrow space more like a two-floor apartment than a house, full of horrors, concluding with a masked man dressed as Leatherface chasing us out with a chainsaw. We laughed guffs full of adrenaline as we made our way down the street. I met all sorts of folks, high school football players headed off on college scholarships and hilarious girls Crystal knew.

And then I met my prom king: Darius Parrish, a chocolate-skinned, baby-faced boy Crystal had graduated with. He was rolling with a crew of guys. I was instantly drawn to his low southern drawl; he sounded similar to the guys in Atlanta but with a bit of Geechee in his voice. Crystal told me Darius was a gentleman. And he was laid back and not playing the scene like his more boisterous homeboys. He was sharp-dressed too, wearing a crisp black-and-white-striped Polo shirt over a white ribbed tank and some dark-wash jean shorts with creases sharp as razors and a pair of super-clean white sneakers. His voice was so low that I had to lean in to hear him. His breath smelled fresh, like the Doublemint gum he was chewing. We became inseparable, joking lightheartedly and hugging as we took over the street with our massive crew. It felt good to have someone else to talk to because I felt like a permanent third wheel with Crystal and David all booed up.

For the next three days, we partied and bounced around the beach and made beelines through hotel suites and cheap restaurants, binging on McDonald's burgers and crab legs and convenience store junk food and super-size Slurpees, and seeing groups like 112 and Allure in concert. I made several friends, and we exchanged usernames, vowing to add each other as AOL buddies just as soon as we got back to our dial-up connections. I couldn't believe this was my new life.

As it turned out, when I got to Atlanta my new life did prove to be transformative and liberating, if not much like I'd pictured it. Crystal and I didn't end up staying close. We remained acquaintances, occasionally exchanging messages on AOL. We never really fell out, but things between us were never quite the same after our trip. I think David's presence messed up the dynamic between the two of us. Online Crystal presented as lively and social, when in real life she was far more withdrawn, with a natural energy set to a low, intense frequency. I was effervescent and highly social, especially if I liked you. We just could never find equal footing. And David manipulated this difference, halfway nicely, trying to be the good guy and bridge the gap between two such different women, and partly using me to make Crystal feel insecure. The two of them actually broke up shortly thereafter.

Rather than rooming together at Clark Atlanta that fall, I had the en suite single in Beckwith that we had both dreamed of; Crystal was across campus in raggedy Pfeiffer Hall, with the other folks who'd got their housing deposits in late. We crossed paths only once or twice that year, most notably when we were both recognized for making the dean's list. We exchanged pleasantries and vowed to hang out, but we never did. Years later, though, we reconnected on Facebook, and I've enjoyed getting to see her actualized as a gifted visual artist, still very beautiful and stylish, with a headful of violet kinky curls in a punky cut. I guess it's only fitting that our friendship lives on in the digital social space from which it was birthed.

7

Knee-High Boots

I was living my best Nola Darling life my freshman year of college at Clark Atlanta University. Nola is the heroine in Spike Lee's 1986 cult classic film *She's Gotta Have It*, an alluring artist, part of the Brooklyn bohème scene, juggling three lovers who, collectively, pay for her lifestyle and keep her entertained and sexually satisfied while she pours her enthralling life experiences into her art. I fashioned myself as a newly liberated Nola, juggling dates, sliding into booths at the finest ATL restaurants, brushing elbows with celebrities, and partying at the crunkest clubs. It was so grown and sexy.

At least it felt that way.

In reality, it was more drugstore ramen noodles and two-piece "wing-on-wheat" meals from Stegall's (a black-owned, bodega-like store on campus), and occasionally seeing the back of a celebrity's head at the mall. But it *felt* fabulous and exciting. I was mapping my liberation on my own terms.

Atlanta was the buckle of the Bible Belt, steeped in the rich history of the black church. Women dressed in elaborate church "crowns" and conservative dresses and men wore hard-bottom shoes and button-down shirts as they tipped into the early morning Sunday services across the city. But some of these same folks were also tippin' into the nightclubs, trading their A-lined frocks for freakum dresses. I came to love the duality and the openness of black life in Atlanta.

That feeling of freedom is what drew me and some of my high school friends to Atlanta, the home of Freaknik, in the first place. Every year, a few older folks from Fort Wayne would drive down to Atlanta for the legendary Freaknik street party and come back with tales of random hook-ups, public nudity, street drinking, freak dancing, and other debauchery. According to legend, the finest black women in the country danced on cars in coochie cutters and pumps as dudes threw down their best mack daddy lines, while Luke's "I Wanna Rock (Doo Doo Brown)" pumped from the mob of cars that had shut down the city's major intersections. There was no doubt that it was going down in the A-T-L; I had to be there.

Freaknik had virtually died by the time I arrived in Atlanta near the end of the 90s, but the spirit that birthed the party was still crunk. Dad had no clue when he kissed my forehead and reluctantly made the eight-hour solo drive back home with an empty U-Haul that he was dropping his daughter off in hip hop Babylon. Nor did I realize just how sheltered I had been until I was let loose without parental guidance in the black mecca. There was a sea of black folks on the adjoining campuses (Clark Atlanta, Spelman, Morehouse, Morris Brown) that comprised the Atlanta University Center, and in the hood of Southwest Atlanta (nicknamed "the SWATS") that surrounded the campus. For the first time in my life I looked around and saw not a white person in sight. It was surreal.

I knew I was in a whole 'notha world when I saw girls on campus breaking out their stylish knee-high boots at the first sign of fall. The slim-fitting shafts—usually made out of leather or velvet—hug the calves. They create a sleek silhouette that makes the wearer's legs look a mile long. Girls in my high school didn't wear knee-high boots. From a young age we knew that those shoes were on a list of items "too grown" for us, along with fire-red nail polish and lipstick and heavy perfume. According to the churchgoing adults in our young lives, knee-high boots were shoes for club-hopping women, street walkers, strippers, and drug dealers' girlfriends. They said this stuff to deter us from *scandalous* activity, to place big loud warning signs on sin by draping it in recognizable garments. *If you hate sin, don't dress like a sinner.* Now, plenty of adults were wearing the boots, but since we couldn't talk back to or question grown folk, we mostly just left this rather vague line between *grown* and *too grown* alone, giving the occasional side-eye when we knew they couldn't see us.

Mom owned a pair of shiny brown leather knee-high boots with a subtly pointed toe and a modest pointed heel that she wore on occasion, but then she never preached the sartorial gospel of good girl looks. For Mom, it was more about how you wore a garment—since knee-high boots were seen as super sexy, she opted to wear them in conservative colors and silhouettes.

By the time I was in high school, my older cousin Nikia and her friends had graduated into the local nightclub scene. They wore their knee-high boots with short, tight skirts that showed off the dimples in their meaty booties as they bounced between the Legion (a military veterans' post) and Pierre's, the popular nightspots in our factory town, capturing their hot-girl irreverence in overexposed club Polaroids. But most of us high school girls knew that although knee-highs were achingly desirable, they weren't for us, especially not those of us who had plans to go to college. The message that knee-high boots equaled "fast" had been ingrained into our heads: if you ain't tryna "give it up," you got no damn business in knee-high boots—or at the club, for that matter. The odd thing was, of course, that although we weren't wearing knee-high boots, most of us were having sex, and some of us were having babies. Fort Wayne was a crumple of contradictions like that.

The boys didn't get so much grief over their clothes, though the restrictions they did have said a lot about the small-minded culture in Fort Wayne. Boys were told to pull up their sagging pants. Why? Because sagging was a sign that you were gay. Apparently, it dated back to some old prison myth. Unlike us girls, though, they were never told that they needed to curb their *heterosexual* desires; boys never got branded "fast." No, they were warned about the dangers of dating a fast-tailed *girl* who would try to get them caught up with an STD, or worse, a baby.

Those types of stories about the good and the bad girl ordered our social life in Fort Wayne. I wasn't a good girl; that ship had long since sailed for me. And what I now understood was that being fast wasn't just about sex. It had little to do with sex, because not all girls who were openly having sex were made to wear the scarlet *F*. Being fast had as much to do with the fact that some adults feared that your curiosity about "grown folks' dealings" was too dangerous for your own good, a curiosity that would render the adults powerless to protect you from the world. Some also feared that you would outpace them in life, learn more, experience more. And if you did that, how could they ever communicate with you, relate to you, manage you, control you? So they hurled out words like *fast*, which stung when they hit, more so out of their own fear and insecurities than as a way to name our "bad" behavior. Some of our folks would rather throw us girls away than grapple with their own brokenness.

In any case, in Fort Wayne I'd always been seen as too grown: I'd been born weird and unrelatable because of my parents' dashiki politics; I was too inquisitive for my own good; I had already lived on my own in New England; I had a kid; I spoke my mind, even to adults. But although I was the epitome of fast, I was also ambitious and college-bound, so I, subconsciously, still held on to the idea that knee-high boots weren't for me.

Our parents weren't all the way wrong when they linked knee-high boots with nightclubs and sexual freedom. They came of age in the 1960s, when boots were the symbol of the sexual revolution. It started in the early 1960s when designers Beth Levine and André Courrèges helped elevate boots to the realm of high fashion. Levine popularized the stiletto heel (even making the boots Nancy Sinatra wore in her "These Boots Are Made for Walking" video), while Courrèges was known for creating a low-heeled, white leather ankle boot. Of course, boots of all heights have been circulating in fashion for centuries. Levine and Courrèges got their inspiration emulating the looks that stylish women and nonbinary femmes were already wearing in dive bars and discotheques. Using pricey textiles and slapping their names on the labels, they reinvented street styles for the runway, just like Courrèges had done with other popular youth styles that black women across Africa, South America, and the Caribbean had been wearing for decades, like miniskirts and hot pants.

Designers create desire, but most folks can't afford their wares. So black women and femmes remixed the high-end boot designs. Some who were savvy with a sewing machine made their own by stitching stretchy fabric to a pair of high heels. By the mid-60s, pleather and vinyl Courrèges knockoffs and similar styles were visible in the hippest nightclubs and basement parties around the world. Nightclub owners decided they could draw even more male and masculine-presenting clientele if they hired dancers to wear the boots and short skirts as they gyrated on tables and high perches around the club. These dancers, and the boots they wore, were given the label "gogo," or "go-go." *À gogo* means "abundance" or "galore" in French. After the Parisian club Whisky à Gogo, which opened at the end of World War II, became famous for its heady mix of spirits, fashion, and dancing, go-go also became slang for the high, fast-paced energy of the nightclub. The Chicago Whisky a Go-Go, launched in the late 1950s, was the first such club to open in the United States, followed by one in Los Angeles in the mid-1960s that became just as popular as the original. Go-go dancers were exotic dancers who, unlike strippers, didn't get totally naked but often danced for tips and created their own costumes and personas. They became a popular featured attraction in both straight and queer club scenes.

As the 60s melded into the 70s, the boots got more and more

dramatic: the heels soared higher, lengthening the leg's silhouette, and the shaft of the boot climbed up and up, eventually coming over the knee to the upper thigh, drawing the onlooker's eye to trace the leg all the way up to damn near the crotch area. The boots were now main features in porn films and adult magazines. And it was common to see hookers sporting knee- and thigh-high boots in gritty urban dramas. Club culture was pushing the envelope in other ways too: dancers started performing topless, with the tightest of hot pants and the tallest of boots covering their lower halves as they twirled and popped in metal cages suspended from the ceiling. Tamer versions of go-go dancers appeared on *Hullabaloo* and *Soul Train*— but our parents' first reference point for knee-high boots was the image of the erotic go-go dancer and the street walker, and that's what stuck for them.

Here I was now in college—three decades after the first go-go boots became popular—seeing all the black girls break out their knee-high boots like they hadn't gotten the memo that knee-high boots were for hoochies and porn stars. They wore the boots with skintight designer jeans, miniskirts, and maxi skirts, with fitted tops and blazers. They had boots in every color, textile, and heel and toe shape imaginable. I had no clue knee-high boots were so versatile. But I was discovering that there was a *lot* about fashion and makeup that I didn't know. Every day I was learning the name of some new designer I'd never heard of before. My latest: Moschino. A pretty mocha-complexioned girl with a long doobie wrap who was in my public speaking class had that name written in large, black block letters across her gray belly top as she strutted across campus in stiletto-heeled boots and skinny jeans. *How do you even pronounce that name?* I thought as I saw her. I tried to sound it out in my head: *Moo-SHEE-no? Muh-SHINE-oh?* I settled on *Muh-SHINE-oh.* It was a good thing I didn't say it out loud and embarrass myself because I later learned that it was pronounced *Mos-KEE-no.* Then I remembered the lyrics from one of my favorite Queen Latifah songs, a 1996 diss record, "Name Callin'":

> We know, bootleg, Korean-coppin schemin hoe
> I know it's bootleg cause they misspelled Moschino (It says "Maskino"!)

On the track, Queen clearly pronounces the brand *Mos-KEE-no.* I had no real context back then to understand what she was talking about anyway, so I just rapped along, guessing that the Queen was talkin' bout something righteous. Come to find out, she was referring to a girl rockin' an Asian knockoff of the Italian haute couture label. The pretty girl in my class might have been wearing a knock-off shirt for all I knew, but with the tight jeans that reminded me of the Guess jeans we all wanted in the 80s and them high boots, she had the look *down!*

Fashion was everything in the Atlanta University Center, and every clan had its own look. You had the girls who rocked African prints and head wraps who read poetry and adopted African names after they were initiated into Yoruba spiritual communities. There were the girls who modeled in all of the campus fashion shows (fashion shows were a huuuuuge deal in the AUC), who wore designer clothes and MAC makeup. (I had no idea what this "MAC" was; over winter break I had to ask cousin Nikia for guidance, and she helped me select my first non-drugstore makeup.)

The folks in Greek-letter organizations—who were also the campus queens and kings and student government officers—tended to dress *professionally*, the girls in Ann Taylor skirt suits and fitted sweaters, the guys in conservative sweaters, stylish corduroys and khakis, and pea coats. These were kids from old money black families who vacationed in Hilton Head and "the Vineyard" and had been a part of Jack and Jill—and then there were the folk who dressed the part because they aspired to join the black bourgeoisie. Who knew that knee-high boots could also be paired with a two-piece skirt suit?

Then there was the black queer/punk set with tons of piercings and tattoos. Their style was a bit more anarchist, nonconforming: "edgy" they call it in the fashion world. Some of them rocked knee-high boots too—guys and girls and folks who identified as some other space on the gender spectrum. And when they weren't on campus they hung out in Little Five Points, an eclectic, alternative neighborhood east of downtown, or at some of the black gay bars that played house and sissy bounce music. They were a smaller clique, but I was taken with their unapologetic style. I wanted to get a tongue piercing so badly. I even rode the MARTA bus all the way to Little Five Points to get one, but I guess I wasn't quite ready to let go of my Midwestern notions of propriety. The black woman driving the empty bus easily talked me out of it.

There were the girls whose fashions were super over-the-top and elaborate, who wore rib-cage-grazing weaves, huge earrings and chunky jewelry, neon colors, Crayola crayon lipstick, and wild-colored acrylic nails that curved like sloth claws. This set tended to be from Detroit and Memphis and New Orleans and the neighborhoods that comprised the SWATS. The bougie girls thought these girls were ghetto; they were being snide. But ghetto was actually *in* in the late 90s, used to describe much of the hottest, most outlandish, chinchilla-fur-and-diamond-chain-drippin' hip hop fashion. We were living in the ghetto fabulous era, where excess was in like it had been in the early 80s, according to Puffy, Lil' Kim, Cam'ron, Gangsta Boo, and rapper Ras Kass, whose song "Ghetto Fabulous" came out that year.

The point here was clear: whatever you wore, your look *had* to be on point. And knee-high boots paired well with nearly everything. My look was not on point—only blunt edges. I didn't own anything that put me squarely in any of those camps. I had a secondhand Ralph Lauren garment or two that my mother had let me have and a couple of tops from the Limited and Express that I had purchased with my graduation money. My encounter with Crystal in Myrtle Beach that past summer had taught me that I needed to step my game up at least a little bit before I hit campus. It was settled, I needed a pair of knee-high boots.

I started saving what scraps of money I could, but it wasn't coming together very fast. Enter a guy named Reggie. I was still using my AOL account and meeting people in AUC chat rooms. Reggie went to Morehouse and lived off campus. He picked me up in his Acura and whisked me off to Cobb County one afternoon. Reggie was just dark enough that he wasn't light skinned but was light enough and vain enough that he described himself as light skinned because he thought it came with privilege—never mind the fact that light-skinned brothas had been out of style since the 80s. His hair wasn't quite curly, but if he could've willed his kinks to curl up like

80s R&B cutie Al B. Sure! he absolutely would have. I should've known that he thought of himself as a pretty boy, a member in training of Kappa Alpha Psi Fraternity who never made the line, because his AOL handle had "fine" in it (something only a pretty boy would do). IRL, he wasn't all that fine. I was slightly disappointed.

On the drive to Cumberland Mall, he played the role of the elder Atlanta statesman, schooling me on the politics of the AUC, the dos and don'ts, how to make a *good* name for myself, when to move off campus, and such. When I asked how he afforded to live alone in Austell, he told me about his doctor father and the middle-class black community he grew up in in Nashville. These were the type of folks who would never dare name their kids Tanisha or Ja-Marcus. I met so many Averys, Millicents, Benjamins, and Gray-sons; names I would've considered white just a few months earlier. These AUC kids with fancy surnames like Baptiste and Sinclair and St. James-Toussaint had parents financing their entire lifestyle as they pushed daddy's Benz around campus. (I didn't know anything about cars until I came to Clark. All of a sudden, I was speaking of Mercedes-Benz classes and BMW series.) And lineage mattered in these odd ways to these black folks. They put a premium on being born into a free black family, meaning your family didn't have slave roots; being part of the most elite chapters of Jack and Jill; and having mothers who were Links. They were like the real-life Banks family from *The Fresh Prince of Bel-Air*. The whole performance made me uneasy.

My parents had given me a very different attitude. My dad drove nice cars and had made his way into corporate jobs with large bonus checks, and of course my mom had her family full of HBCU graduates who had pledged Greek organizations and held memberships in the NAACP and such. My family owned property, and we'd owned horses since I was six. I grew up riding. I spent many days after school mucking out stalls in the hand-me-down English riding boots given to me by one of the best teen riders at our barn—the fact that Mom called it a barn and not a stable was an indicator of how disinvested she was in the fancy labels. I never thought to stake claim to these markers of *elite* class to reposition myself in the campus hierarchy. I never even saw those things as high class. At all. But Reggie did. His pronouncements on class anxiety created an emotional distance between us as wide as the space between our car seats. By the time we pulled up at the mall, I was thoroughly exhausted by his Ralph Lauren chatter.

We strolled around the corridors of Cumberland as Reggie led me over to the cologne counters and explained how he only wore Issey Miyake, Gucci Envy, and Bvlgari (which I struggled to pronounce). I was from the world of Cool Water and Jōvan Musk, Royal Copenhagen, Drakkar Noir, and Joop!, so his talk of high-end designer fragrances was lost on me. I spotted a Bakers, the discount shoe store that I had purchased some of my cutest shoes from over the years. Reggie wasn't impressed but he entertained my whim and followed me into the store. The girls in my dorm who did their shopping at the upscale Phipps Plaza would've turned up their noses too. I suddenly felt like Julia Roberts's character Vivian in *Pretty Woman*—the provincial girl who came from nothing, being squired around by the wealthy, worldly guy with everything. I immediately rushed to a pair of chocolate-brown leather, knee-high boots with a square toe and chunky heel. They would match everything in my wardrobe! I looked at the price tag. They were $89.99. I knew I didn't really have the money to buy them, but if I was playing the role of Vivian I might as well try the shoes on. I had the clerk bring over a pair in a size 9. I removed one of the boots from the crunchy white paper they were covered in and plunged my hand down into the shaft of the boot to feel for stuffing wadded up in the toe before slipping my opaque-stockinged foot into the boot. I zipped it up slowly before standing up and walking around the store, my gait uneven because the heel on my own shoe was much shorter, leaving me to trot like a wounded mare. "Should I get them?" I asked Reggie as I passed him on one of my laps from the chair to the mirror. "The quality isn't very good" was the first thing he could muster. I didn't know much about quality and really didn't give two shits about it. At nineteen, everything was quick and disposable. But I only had a couple hundred dollars in my bank account that had to last most of the semester, and with tax those shoes would eat up a hundred, so I decided against it. "If you want them, I'll buy them for you," Reggie said nonchalantly.

Here I was doing mental mathematics trying to figure out how many packs of ramen I'd have to eat if I spent a hundred dollars to look like the fashionistas on campus, and this veritable stranger was offering to buy my boots like it was nothing. "It's up to you," he said, seeing me contemplating his proposition. The nicest thing I had been gifted up to that point was a Nautica jacket (probably stolen) that didn't fit, given to me the year before by a dude who was part of a clique called the "Nauti Boys." And, really, he more loaned it to me to wear around as a sign that I was his girl. I said yes to Reggie's offer before I really took the time to weigh the price tag *this* offer came with. I wanted those boots so badly. Reggie whipped out his blue Wachovia debit card; I told myself he surely had the money in his account, the way he talked. The payment went through on the first swipe. And the store clerk placed my new boots in a huge Bakers bag.

We left the mall and headed over to the Cheesecake Factory for a late lunch. The Cheesecake Factory was a *thing* in Atlanta. I would hear the girls in the dorms coming back from dates, getting dropped off in a Lexus or Acura or Mustang, saying, "Girrrrrl, he took me to the Cheesecake Factory," like it was Buckingham Palace. If it wasn't Cheesecake, it was Shark Bar or hip hop legend Puffy's brand-new restaurant, Justin's. Here I was now for the first time at the palatial Cheesecake Factory, with its gaudy interior design that looked like a mix between an Applebee's and the Versace mansion. At first I didn't think this was a date, but now with the shoes and the promise of cheesecake for dessert I started to feel like it was. I didn't have romantic feelings for Reggie. I doubt he had them for me either—but here he was shelling out what to me felt like a lot of money.

What I didn't quite get about this "date," or whatever it was, was that in Atlanta, this type of thing is just another part of the hustle. In other words: folks be tryna get they paper *and* get they freak on . . . and in some cases, get they paper *while* gettin' they freak on, which also meant that sometimes they had to *spend* some paper in order to get they freak on.

At first I was just enthralled by the pace of Atlanta. It wasn't fast like New York, but it wasn't as dull as Fort Wayne. Dullness has a way of making things feel slow, like they're moving at a snail's pace. My college friends from New York told me that New York was a hustler's city as well. But there, everyone has somewhere to be and very little time to get there. You gotta hurry up and hustle. Transactions happen quickly. No one has time for pleasantries. Customer service in the ways we define it in the Midwest was nonexistent. In Atlanta, the hustle wasn't about time like that. Things moved just slow enough that you got a good look at them as they moved past. It's about sitting in an experience and savoring it, letting it marinate, letting it develop its complex black southern cosmopolitan flavor.

But the slow-cooker culture didn't mean that folks wasn't on they grind. College girls took shifts at the Blue Flame and other local strip clubs, grinding on ball players and rappers to hustle up enough money for tuition, rent, and the occasional designer handbag. The bougie girls did the same, only it was their parents who were doing the trickin'. Wannabe hip hop artists swarmed the campus record store when stars like Jay-Z, Outkast, and Lauryn Hill visited that fall, trying to push mixtapes into their hands. Folks in the projects surrounding the AUC campuses hustled the college students, sometimes even robbing us of shoes and jewelry and bank cards. The point was: everybody had a hustle, and you were either hustlin' or getting hustled.

Reggie's game was typical: *cakin'* was part of the culture. All the dudes knew you had to show women you had a bag and were willing to come up off it, buying her designer shoes and tennis bracelets and Fendi bags and paying rent and car notes. In exchange, she might offer up sex and companionship. Snagging a baller, and figuring out just how much you could get before he expected sex, was akin to a work-study job for some girls, which was why girls were always getting dropped off at the dorm in luxury vehicles. Your average college dude knew he was competing with guys who had way more bank. So Reggie laid out his bona fides early to let me know he was sittin' on a little something. It was the only way he thought he *might could* get some ass. He didn't. I hadn't yet figured out how this all worked, so his play was lost on me.

The sex-for-gifts hustle wasn't for me anyway. The seasoned hustlers in my dorm thought I was being dumb, but I was enjoying myself and having plenty of sex for free. Atlanta was a raunchy playground for sheltered kids like me on the brink of adulthood. And everybody was just so damn fine. I swear some of the most gorgeous girls and guys went to school in the AUC. And if you were willing to venture a bit further afield, there was a whole other pool at Georgia State and Georgia Tech. And I even bumped into the occasional Kennesaw State student at a club or some such party, as we grinded on each other while Juvenile's "Back That Azz Up" blasted through the speakers, hoping to exchange numbers before the DJ played Three 6 Mafia's "Tear Da Club Up" and folks started doing just that, busting up the party. And that was just the student populations. It was all so hard to resist.

For the first time, I didn't feel like a weirdo who'd never fit the only mold there was. In Atlanta, I could make choices. I could pick out the pieces of who I was and who I wanted to be, especially when it came to my sexuality. My queer family members and friends back home had to live secret lives, sneaking into the gay bars and drag shows on Pearl Street or hooking up 'round midnight in Foster Park. I knew it existed on some low frequency because Mom worked security at some of the gay bars and at the (white) PRIDE parade, but there was no visible black queer culture in Fort Wayne for me to envision myself in. And as recently as Myrtle Beach, there was still a lot of uneasiness in my efforts to claim my gender and sexuality.

In Atlanta, I was finally comfortable. I started to make sense to myself and the fact that, at nineteen, I never saw children and marriage—all the things that society tells women we should want—as central to my life. It wasn't that I didn't want a family (I mean, I already had a son whom I felt a nagging guilt about for letting my mom raise him while I was off sowing my proverbial wild oats in college). I just didn't want my life to revolve around *having* to have a family. I was more interested in having a fabulous career, where I could travel and be part of a black expat community in Paris or Berlin, like Zora Neale Hurston and James Baldwin and Audre Lorde and the other folks who seemed queer, sexually fluid, and free. I was learning about in my courses. I didn't want to *be* a man, but I wanted to live the way the world allows men to live: with power and choices and freedom. One of my Baltimore homegirls on the step team nailed it when she told me I was an "aggressive femme." That was one of the first times a label seemed to tell me something useful about myself. Atlanta could also be a very hostile space for black queer and trans-gender folks, but it was there that I learned a language to define the beautifully complex spaces between male and female and gay and straight, and that let me express myself in a fuller, deeper way.

So I had my new knee-high boots, a layered weave, and an elevated new approach to makeup too, and I was roaming the black mecca with an empowering new sense of self. But I was still broke. And that's a big problem in a place like Atlanta, where material life matters so much. I was hanging with a family friend named Ayanna one day, and she offered a solution to my problem. Ayanna was exactly one month older than me and a ton more "worldly." She knew well the ways of the city. Ayanna was born in Chicago and had been living in

Atlanta since she was a teenager, a pampered princess in the black suburbs. At nineteen she still lived at home, but she had plenty of independence. She was a tall, dark brown, curvy girl—with a flat tummy and thick breasts and thighs that Atlanta cats liked. She wore long weaves, had a tongue ring and a barbed-wire tattoo that went around the fleshy meat of her upper arm, and kept her acrylic nails freshly filed. She could rival any of the vixens who were becoming mainstays in hip hop videos. And most of her friends could too. Ayanna was never really oriented toward school and decided young that she could use her gorgeous body, pretty face, and baby voice to hustle whatever her parents wouldn't get her. She worked odd jobs and went in and out of community college classes while she networked with other aspiring models, dancers, and makeup artists, folks on the fringes of Atlanta's entertainment industry.

Hanging with Ayanna helped me get away from campus and learn about Atlanta, beyond the projects of the SWATS. I was far more square than most of her friends, and I just couldn't keep up with their way of hooking dudes. I was way too direct to play the sweet "companion" role that they worked. But she took pity on me, perhaps seeing me as a project, and kept my weaves looking good, gave me fashion advice, and let me tag along when she hung out with C-list celebs. One time, she took me to Mark and Red's house in Stone Mountain. The light-skinned brothers were members of Another Bad Creation, who had been one of my fave R&B boy groups back in the day. Now, she was gonna help me get my money right, with a job at the Gold Club.

I knew the name from folks around school. The Gold Club was one of the most exclusive mixed-race strip clubs in the city. A gentleman's club, they called it. Apparently, all of the high rollers—

ballplayers, rappers, high-level drug dealers, and crime bosses—went to the Gold Club when they wanted a more exclusive experience than Magic City or Blue Flame offered. I knew I wasn't prepared to be a stripper, so I was relieved when Ayanna said I'd work as a hostess, which was a semi-classy way of saying "bottle girl" or "waitress." Long before bottle girls became minor celebrities on Instagram, they were rock stars on the Atlanta strip club scene, wielding desire and a modicum of power. Ayanna had done a stint as a Gold Club hostess and claimed she brought home $200 or more in tips every night, courtesy of the ballers who liked to trick off on the scantily clad sexpots who popped their corks and kept the bubbly flowing. I didn't even have $200 in my bank account, so the thought of making $200 *a night* was appealing. Ayanna was trying to save up for a red convertible Chrysler Sebring, so she decided to go with me to my "interview" to get her old job back.

It seemed that half the work at a gentleman's club was personal maintenance, and that was a hidden drain on your tips. Dancers and hostesses had to keep their weaves tight, bodies waxed and smelling good, and nails done. They even brought in professional makeup artists to "beat" the dancers' faces. Dancers had to look the part even when they weren't on shift. On campus, you'd see them in their trendy clothes and spike-heeled boots, strutting down the promenade with a clockable air of sexual confidence.

Things weren't as strict for hostesses, but they still had a standard to maintain. Ayanna said my face was pretty enough that I would get good tips—which was also a nice way of saying that it would make up for my lack of curves. Hostesses had to be charming masters of suggestion and manipulation, liaising between patrons and bartenders, remembering patrons by name and flirting with them, catering to their needs, and generally keeping them liquored up and spendy. The tipsier the patrons were, the more money they'd spend on bottles (nearly $400 a pop) and dances ($20 for a lap dance, $200 for private time in one of the back rooms).

To become a hostess, I'd have to front a chunk of cash for the work permit and $250 for the uniform—a black corset with bloomer-type bottoms, black thigh-high stockings with a garter attachment, and black stilettos. I would be in the hole half a *stack* before I even worked one shift. Ayanna promised to cover me, and pitched it as an investment in my future; I would quickly make that money back and then some, she assured me. I wondered who had given her that speech. It sounded quite compelling—that's how a place like Atlanta gently pimps you into the hustle. In the hood, everyone focuses on how boys get lured into the drug game. For women, the strip club scene is the equivalent. Dancers make good, quick cash money. They have the fancy cars and the dopest clothes. They set the fashion trends in the hood that the rest of the world ends up adopting. Plus, although turning tricks in the back rooms or taking clients to nearby hotels was a liability, stripping in Atlanta was perfectly legal, so it didn't come with the same risks as drug running. Girls in the club world loved the flexibility of the job: you could design your own work schedule and stop and start when you wanted. For women who were dancing full time, not as a side hustle or a way to supplement what mommy and daddy were giving them (which few folks were doing), dancing gave them more autonomy than low-wage retail or food-and-hospitality service jobs did. And the women who were good at the hustle, running their financial affairs and interactions with clients like bawse chicks, did make good money.

Ayanna and I rolled up to the gold-and-jet-black club around noon. The parking lot was relatively empty, save a luxury vehicle or two. I had never been to a strip club before. I had watched an HBO special on strippers and imagined it would smell like perspiration and baby powder and Victoria's Secret Amber Romance lotion. And glitter. Tons of glitter. Inside it was dim enough that my eyes took time to adjust. There was one woman dancing in a front room area, seemingly more for her own amusement than for tips because the space was empty. But the DJ was still spinning some kind of smoothed-out hip hop, and the neon signs were lit and the colored lights made wild patterns on the wall. The carnival was open, even though there was no one on the rides. I was kind of relieved. I needed to ease my way into the strip club scene.

Ayanna sauntered over to her homeboy Keith, the hiring manager, switching her booty in her tight pants as her stiletto boots click-clacked on the tiled floor. She said something to him in a low tone before tossing her weaved head back and laughing loudly in her little baby voice. Watching her work this hustle, I forgot that she wasn't even twenty years old yet. She seemed like a seasoned pro. She waved me over, introducing me as her "sister" who was looking for work. "Your sister, huh?" he asked as he let his eyes roll down the surface of my body. I shifted uncomfortably. As instructed, I had worn the "sexiest" thing in my closet, which amounted to a low-cut black top, black ponte pants from Express, and some black heeled boots from my step team's homecoming show. I looked more like a MAC makeup artist than a cocktail waitress. I introduced myself, speaking in a low, sultry tone, letting my hazel eyes linger on him a second longer than would be professional in a corporate work environment. Keith saw through me but he let me keep up my sexy ruse.

I followed him over to some couches that sat on low-pile black carpet, where undoubtedly countless professional athletes had received lap dances from oiled-up dancers with D-cup implants and juicy asses. He started the interview asking, "How old are you?" I responded to his initial question about my age a little too tersely to be believable: "Twenty-one." My nineteen-year-old armpits started to perspire a bit as I waited to hear his response to my blatant lie. Please don't let him ask to see my ID. Ayanna had promised that he wouldn't, but the police officer's daughter in me said that there was no way this man would give an underage girl a job handling alcohol in a twenty-one-and-over club. He just said, "Okay," and moved on with the interview. Damn! Again, I realized just how naïve I was. Keith continued with a series of questions, most of which I can't remember. But one stuck in my mind because it showed me what kind of boss he'd be: "How many glasses are in a bottle of champagne?" Was this strip club *Jeopardy*? "Seven," I guessed. "No," he said firmly. "The answer is five." He went on to explain condescendingly how a hostess needed to know this in order to make the right pours per bottle so as to not short the house or make the customers complain that they didn't get the right number of pours. It made sense, but his tone made it clear that he thought of his underlings as pretty idiots to his patriarchal wisdom. And I wasn't here for it. The nerd in me was pissed that I hadn't had the answer to win Gold Club trivia, but it didn't take a genius to memorize how many pours were in a bottle of Moët.

Somehow, I passed this interview and was hired on the spot. Ayanna was hype, but I was torn about taking the job. I called my mom that night, and she listened, never sounding angry or judgmental. She actually opened up about her life, before me, when she worked as a bartender after she dropped out of college. She hipped me to what it's like to work in a nightclub, the pros and the cons. The pros: quick money, every night is different, flexibility, the drama and excitement. The cons: the drama and excitement, patrons thinking they own you and demeaning you, and tension with coworkers over money and popularity. I appreciated her genuineness. I now understood why my cousin Nikia and other girls in the hood felt comfortable coming to her with all their drama. If only I had known this earlier. If only I could've seen her as more than a disciplinarian, I could've saved myself a lot of grief over the years. I hung up from the call loving my mom more, realizing that she was once a young, silly girl trying to be an adult too.

I ended up disappointing Ayanna and passing on the job. It was for the best. A couple years later, the Gold Club was embroiled in a huge scandal—with prostitution, money laundering, and credit card fraud allegations. For their part, hostesses were being instructed to do some pretty shady stuff, like get patrons so drunk that they were running up $10,000 tabs, even though they weren't coherent enough to really consent to the charges, or pour a couple of drinks from the bottle and then spill the rest onto the carpet so the bottle would run out quicker (So much for needing to know how many pours were in a bottle!). Instead, I took a minimum-wage gig, shuffling around in my brown knee-high boots, slangin' body scrubs and lotions at the Bath & Body Works in Lenox Square Mall, in the bougie Buckhead area.

After a year of racking up debt in the black mecca, I decided to transfer home for my sophomore year. I didn't want to leave Atlanta, but that quiet nag of not raising Malik full time had turned into a cacophonous ringing that I couldn't silence. Perhaps it was all of the advice from my chosen mothers who had pleaded with me: "Go get your son. He needs *you*." Perhaps it was my steady diet of Lauryn Hill's "To Zion" from *The Miseducation of Lauryn Hill* album, which dropped that first week of fall classes freshman year. That song had been building my pride in being a mother and helping me truly see my son as a blessing, while simultaneously reducing me to tears. But how could I reconcile the new self I had discovered in Atlanta with the old self I had left in Fort Wayne? I dreaded going back to Indiana, starting all over, and at a white school at that. But Indiana University was offering me a full ride; it would help ease the financial burden my father was currently helping me carry.

I set up an apartment for Malik and me and tried to adjust to my new reality in Bloomington, Indiana. My family support system was nearly three hours up the highway. Still, I somehow managed to juggle the demands of motherhood and the rigors of my schoolwork. I scratched and clawed my way onto the dean's list and earned the respect of my professors, who allowed me to bring Malik to class on days when his school was closed.

Like my mother had done years before when she was a student at IU, I joined a sorority and became a campus leader and all that. One day, we were at a sorority event and I peeled off my baggy gray sweatshirt. One of the girls in the sorority, who was a year older than me and light-years more churchy, stared at the t-shirt I had on underneath. "Is that a *man* on her shirt?" she yelled out. "That's a *man* on her shirt," she said, answering her own question. I had to look down because I didn't even remember which shirt I had put on. There was a screen-printed image of Tula, one of the most legendary drag queens in Indiana. My mom had given me this shirt after she judged a drag competition that Tula hosted in Fort Wayne. The other older girls started walking up to me, grabbing and pulling on my shirt, laughing and teasing me for wearing a shirt with a *man* on it. I loved my Tula shirt, in part because my mother had given it to me, but also because my freedom to wear that shirt in public had come with all of the lessons I had learned in Atlanta. I fixed my mouth to yell back, explaining drag culture and gender and the bigger, wider, queerer world I knew existed. But I knew that would be pointless. I just stared at the girl who'd started this mess, never breaking her gaze, until she and the other girls shut up. They moved on to some other stereotypically mean sorority-girl conversation. This was my new life. I had clicked my knee-high boots and ended up back in socially conservative Indiana. At least I was reunited with my son.

8

Bamboo Earrings

The heels of my cheap, plastic-soled, pink thong stiletto sandals clacked in a staccato rhythm as I stumbled down the dark hallway of Club Cheetah, the venue Jay-Z rapped about in his hit song "I Just Wanna Love U (Give It 2 Me)." My beltless Charlotte Russe bell bottoms were starting to sag after a long night of whining, pepper seeding, and droppin' it to Chaka Demus and Pliers' classic "Murder She Wrote" and Khia's "My Neck, My Back (Lick It)." Every few stumbly steps, I yanked my pants up to cover my exposed blush-colored lace thong. I knew the pants were slightly

ill-fitting when I bought them, but desire compelled me to purchase them anyway. I found the hole that they called a bathroom
and somehow managed to steady myself in the grimy stall long
enough to "go," then peered at my image in the smeared bathroom
mirror above the sink as I washed my hands. I recognized my
dusty-pink, slouchy bohemian top and center-parted cornrows that
were braided up into a high ponytail with a poof of crinkly weave
hair cascading from them. My face, though, didn't look like my
own. It was slightly puffy and contorted: eyes glassy, jaws slack. I was
tipsy. Okay, I was drunk . . . and in New York City for the first
time.

This vacation was desperately needed. I'd moved back to Fort
Wayne after college and had started one of those terrible-paying-
yet-rewarding jobs, teaching first grade at an inner-city charter
school on the same side of town I grew up on. I had made myself
a little social circle of other folks who worked in the education
field and a few other college-degree-type jobs. From this vantage
point, I was seeing a slightly more progressive aspect of my factory
town—it wasn't quite as stifling as it was when I was a teenager. I
could imagine how my parents had felt in the 80s when they had
ascended to Fort Wayne's so-called black middle class. But day to
day, my routine was mundane: mornings that began before dawn,
pre-semester course prep and staff meetings, followed by forgetta-
ble dinners in front of the police-procedural television show du
jour. I quickly realized: adulting was boring as hell.

One evening, my boarding school friend Shandrica called. Our
friendship had survived the teen years with letters and phone calls,
and then we got email—but we still liked to mail each other real
letters from time to time, occasionally including pictures so that we

could see how each of us was changing over time. Shandrica had just graduated from an Ivy League university and had moved back to New York, her native city, for an internship at one of the big investment banking firms. "Girl, what are you gonna do for your birthday?" she asked. I realized that in my haste to move home and find a job I hadn't even thought about the fact that my birthday was quickly approaching. "Well, you know you always have an open invitation to come kick it in N-Y-C!" She had extended this offer before, but this time it made all the sense in the world: it could be my last college-era hoorah before my school year started and adulting fully set in like rigor mortis. And just like that, I decided I'd spend my twenty-second birthday in the city, doing the black Carrie Bradshaw thing with Shan and her homegirls.

This time around, I felt legit grown as I packed my luggage and my modest makeup collection: mostly CoverGirl and a few of the MAC products I'd been using since my Clark Atlanta days. The bohemian look was *in* that summer, and I was doing it to *death*. I packed a knee-length denim skirt with a camel-colored, ruffled, off-the-shoulder top; my denim bell bottoms; and a host of other boho-chic tops, large hoop earrings, and stone necklaces. I was young and employed, with my own apartment and a modest bank account. Young, broke, and fabulous, as Suze Orman calls it.

New York City was a mecca for the hip hop generation. Traveling there was a hajj, a spiritual pilgrimage, of sorts. I was definitely intimidated, but I was ready for a real encounter. I flew out of the Fort Wayne International Airport, with its dozen gates and two baggage claim belts, and into bustling LaGuardia Airport, which was massive in comparison. "Oh my gawd!" I screamed when I finally laid eyes on my dear friend. Shandrica and I hugged tight, holding one another a second for every year we'd gone without seeing each other. We had changed so much since we were fifteen—the two tomboys in "Brandy braids" and baggy jeans. We were each now on our own journey to develop our unique performance of feminine professionalism. Shandrica had let her relaxed sandy-brown hair grow down to the middle of her back and was wearing fitted dresses and heels or tight-fitting designer jeans and tank tops. She had always downplayed her natural good looks in high school. Now, here she was looking like a Wall Street J.Lo. I loved her style evolution and the confidence that seemed to come with it.

When I had a moment to take in the city, a wave of nostalgia washed over me: I was in the land of bamboo earrings. Seeing that black girl flair on every corner gave me all the feels. Bamboo earrings had been *the* earrings of the late 1980s and early 90s. Every black and brown girl and femme wanted a pair, but you had to be the *flyest* of the fly girls to even attempt to rock them. If you had a pair of bamboos but the rest of your outfit was wack, you'd be exposed as a fashion fraud.

The earrings ain't really made of bamboo, of course. Some folk paid top dollar for the real gold earrings, the kind that were so heavy they made your earlobes sag. But there was a range in quality, believe me! And most folks where I'm from were buying the cheap ones, made of low-quality, gold-plated metal. The even cheaper ones would be plastic with metallic gold paint that starts to flake off a few days after you buy them. Bamboos are like their namesake in that they are hollow and have distinct joints. Those joints are what make a pair of bamboo earrings stand out from any other oversize hoop. There's a bunch of other popular styles of the huge earrings that we descriptively call "doorknockers": there's shrimp, dolphins (that look like two dolphins kissing), triangles, trapezoids, hearts, and so forth.

In any shape, rocking a pair of doorknockers gives you a distinct African or Caribbean flair. Wearing them made us feel both stylish and connected to our roots. At Clark Atlanta, I had learned about how my ancestors in precolonial Africa adorned themselves in gold: elaborate jewelry and gold flakes in their hair. The hip hop generation was reviving this ancient custom, carrying our ancestors' style legacy with us across the diaspora, we believed. Bringing to life the African glamour we'd seen in *Coming to America*'s fictional Zamunda in our real world.

Doorknockers became the consummate earrings of city girls who were pioneering hip hop fashion. Back in the day, all our favorite emcees—all from New York City—wore bamboo earrings in their videos, from Roxanne Shanté to Salt-N-Pepa. So we Indiana girls— far away from the culture's center—couldn't call ourselves hip hop and on trend if we didn't have at least a couple of bamboo earrings in our jewelry box.

Salt-N-Pepa were my style *icons* when I was nine. I asked Mom to get me a pair of bamboo earrings after seeing their "Shake Your Thang" music video. The rap duo was sporting tight-fitted ripped jeans; white cutoff S-N-P t-shirts that showed a sliver of belly skin, with cuts all over the shoulders and arms; matching ball caps with the lid flipped up and S-N-P painted in red letters; alternating red and white socks; and white sneakers. They accentuated their "black girl blonde" asymmetrical *stacked* haircuts with doorknocker earrings and fire-engine-red lipstick. I wanted their entire wardrobe.

The look in this video was instantly inspiring because it had a do-it-yourself feel to it that we Midwestern girls found particularly accessible. In their breakout "Push It" video, Salt-N-Pepa wore custom Dapper Dan jackets. There was no way any kid in a small Rust Belt town was going to access or even really imitate that gear. Our styles were built around buying cheap t-shirts from the dollar store or the Asian-owned flea market shops and piecing together glam looks with the assistance of a hot-glue gun, puffy paint, stencils, and rhinestones and smudging Wet n Wild lipstick on our lips, cheeks, and eyelids (of course, I was so young I could only wear the makeup "for play"). In the "Shake Your Thang" video, they were wearing some real practical black girl shit, an elevated version of the stuff that everyday hood chicks like me and my friends used to sport.

Mom said Salt-N-Pepa's oversize earrings were too grown for me. I whined and pouted. All of the cool older girls in my neighborhood, including my cousin Nikia, were already wearing them with everything from jeans and "college boys" (our name for rugby shirts) to biker shorts, body dresses, and sandals. They were so versatile, equal parts femme and tomboy chic, just like my style. I felt behind, I wasn't on trend. Mom usually cared about that, but she would not be swayed on this one. She bought me S-N-P's new cassette tape *A Salt with a Deadly Pepa* as a consolation prize, and I was appeased. Temporarily.

But my longing for bamboo earrings didn't evaporate. I had been to LA now; I was a girl realizing there was a world beyond my own, a world where black folks were trendsetters and innovators. Bamboo earrings were like amulets that could make me feel creative and free and big city. The rise of hip hop culture was eroding regional fashion identities, feeding black children from place to place with the same vision. We wanted to be transported, or at least connected, to that bigger and unapologetically blacker world. Every girl in Fort Wayne, from the gang affiliated to the middle class, wanted bamboo doorknocker earrings.

By the time LL Cool J dropped "Around the Way Girl" two years later, in 1990, I was old enough for my own pair of bamboo earrings. "*I want a girl with extensions in her hair, bamboo earrings, at least two pair.*" It was this line that made the song a sho' nuff summer anthem. From a young age, black girls are sent messages that we aren't enough, but we also get a lot of messages about how we are *too* much, our lives caught between these contradictions. Most white folks in Fort Wayne didn't understand anything about black culture. The city was so segregated that they didn't really have to interact with us. Black girls in particular, with our elaborate hair-grooming processes and *gawdy* accessories, were foreign to white folks. We knew that these one-generation-removed southern rednecks deemed us loud and excessive and uncouth. Ghetto. They weren't interested in our experiences, just in highlighting what they found exotic. "How did you get your hair to do that?," "Is that your *real* hair?," "Why do you change your hairstyle so much?," and "You don't wash your hair every day?" That was what you'd get from your handful of white classmates, if they weren't ignoring you. White girls and black girls both silently recognized that white girls had the privilege that comes with knowing that their hair and beauty practices are the norm. Meanwhile, we were seen as practicing some odd *minority* shit—even though there were way more of us black girls in the school. The culture of the city was one that devalued our bodies, our hair, our grooming, and no matter how many of us there were, you always knew it.

So when LL rapped about how beautiful our excessive styles

were—he wanted a girl with fake hair and not one but *two* pairs of bamboo earrings—we felt seen and valued and understood. LL strolled through New York, camcorder in hand, capturing on video black and brown women wearing "around the way" looks: big-ass earrings, dookie rope chains, weave ponytails, *stacked* haircuts, belly tops, and bras under airbrushed "jumpers" (what we called overalls) with one strap down. It felt like a black man loved us. And many of us were aching to feel that love—from absentee fathers and brothers as much as from romantic partners. If only he had said "Tanisha" when he did his famous roll call: Lisa, Angela, Pamela, Renee—the names of the girls he tells I love you—I would've adored the song even more. I was not among the chosen. But this song was still a love anthem for me, one of the rare ones that didn't just sexualize us, but celebrated us.

Of course, I didn't mention any of this LL Cool J crush business when my eleven-year-old self returned to Mom with the conversation about getting bamboo earrings. And this time, I was successful. I was going to middle school, and it was time for a rite of passage. One of the big rituals a lot of my peers were using to mark this transition to a new level of grownness was getting a second ear piercing, and Mom was down. So now I not only had permission to buy up a bunch of dope earrings with my allowance, I could elevate to peak fashion status, or go over the top, depending on whose gaze mattered, and rock *two* pairs of bamboo earrings at once. Actually, I was still feeling a little too conservative for the biggest ones, so I opted for the midsize joints. The piercings never healed well; I gave up on them later. But, for now, I was a 'round-the-way girl. At age eleven.

Shandrica had planned an incredible weekend of shopping and clubbing for us for my 2002 B-day weekend. We were gonna hit it all: high-end department stores, vintage boutiques, discount stores, and street stalls slanging knockoff handbags. Here I was on the eve of my twenty-second birthday—the age Salt-N-Pepa were when they recorded "Shake Your Thang"—and I was finally, for real, for real, in the *land* of bamboo earrings. I soaked in the range of styles I saw on the blue A train, following Shandrica's lead through the bewildering system of letters *and* colors *and* numbers in NYC's subway system. For me, it was a big deal when I was old enough to walk the few blocks to school alone. I couldn't fathom traveling to a whole 'nother borough alone as a seven- or eight-year-old like Shandrica had. Perhaps it was this sense of responsibility and spatial mobility at such a young age that made my boarding school friends from New York seem so much more advanced than me. I just tried to mimic Shandrica's pace and fit in, but my small-town origins showed all over my actions: the careless way that I kept money in plain sight, how I got stuck in the turnstile after swiping my MetroCard the wrong way, how I was pushed around in the crowds once we resurfaced near Wall Street. All the bodies, all the honking, all the street food—I was getting why the folks back home were not just in awe but kind of overwhelmed by New York. It was like a foreign country. But I was determined to find a connection with this place.

First up, a designer discount store called Century 21, made famous to outsiders in an episode of *Sex and the City*. According to Shan, Century 21 was a trove of designer fashions at a price point that wouldn't frighten my starter bank account. She started rattling off designers whose names I only knew from *Sex and the City* and hip hop songs: Versace, Manolo Blahnik, Diane von Furstenberg, Christian

Lacroix, Via Spiga, Marc Jacobs, Prada, and Fendi. I only really knew Ralph Lauren, Tommy Hilfiger, Gucci, and Louis Vuitton. Those were the poppin' designer labels back home. Shandrica had all these other favorite high-end brands, but she assured me that we could find all the small-town clothing stars I was acquainted with at Century 21 for good prices.

We walked into Century 21, which was overwhelming in its own way. It looked like a typical department store, with its racks and racks of clothes, shoes, and other accessories. But it had that picked-through, tossed-around feeling of a TJ Maxx or a Value City. Not so much my kind of vibe; clutter makes me anxious. And not what my Midwestern mind would call "cheap" either. But Shandrica was right, there were all sorts of designer duds: Ferragamo, Pucci, Bottega Veneta, Catherine Malandrino. In the shoe department, Shandrica found a cute pair of café au lait–colored sandals that matched her skin tone perfectly. They had a carved wedge heel that came to a point, like wedge stilettos. Thin spaghetti straps crossed over the toes and wrapped around the ankle. They were super sexy. I found a matching pair in a pretty lime-green shade, so now, I had made my first New York City purchase. Shan and me were shoe twins. "Heyyy!" we said as we did a little shoulder shimmy and made plans to wear our shoes at some point over the weekend.

We strolled around Manhattan, window gazing and snacking on Gray's Papaya hot dogs (just a couple of weeks later *Sex and the City* made the stand famous enough that Midwesterners might recognize it). The smells and no-frills attitude of Gray's Papaya reminded me of the hexagon-shaped hot dog stand run by teenagers down the street from my house when I was a kid that sold frothy root beer and anemic hot dogs, where we preteens went for the atmosphere (not so much the food). As I bit into my meal, more bun than hot dog, doused with onions, mustard, and ketchup, New York stopped feeling so foreign, so intimidating.

New Yorkers were so bold and daring in their fashion choices. There was no playbook. There were no rules. You could wear whatever you wanted, dye your hair as many colors as you wanted, wear a ball gown with Adidas and a studded leather jacket just because. Even in Atlanta's rainbow of styles I had never experienced anything so freeing. There was a mix of everything everywhere, but neighborhoods each seemed to have their own special feel too. In SoHo, I saw lots of black: sleek pants and booties, dresses with interesting silhouettes. In the West Village, they wore the whole boho goddess/manufactured grunge look. The Upper West Side was a bit more buttoned up, like old-ish money, in traditional silhouettes but with more colors than SoHo. In Harlem, everything was black and loud: from the music blaring from makeshift kiosks that lined 125th Street to the florid color palettes of garments hanging in the shop windows: geranimal-printed shirts, hard bottoms in colorful snakeskin, West African wax prints. Whether they made a six-figure salary or minimum wage, Harlem's black girls were *stylin' out*; they were not playin'! Their looks were so electric. LL could've shot an updated version of "Around the Way Girl" right there on the corner of 125th and Lenox.

Harlem was definitely the metropole of the land of bamboo earrings. There were entire kiosks devoted to doorknockers: huge earrings in wood, metal, feathers, and printed fabric. *I wanted them all.* I got three pairs after negotiations with an older man from Senegal with rich nut-brown skin, and I promised to bring some home to Mom.

As we walked around Greenwich Village, I had to ask Shandrica,

"What's up with the white girls wearing doorknockers?" It seemed like all the bohemian earth mothers were floating around in bamboo earrings and nameplate necklaces. "Girl, everybody tryna look like Carrie," she said, as she gave me a cynical Brooklyn girl side-eye. *Sex and the City* costume designer Patricia Field had early on dressed the fictional Carrie Bradshaw, newspaper columnist and fashionista, in a 14K gold "Carrie" nameplate necklace that became part of Carrie's funny downtown girl look. And just a year before my pilgrimage to the land of bamboo earrings, Field custom-made a pair of Carrie nameplate bamboo earrings. Just like that, nameplates and bamboo earrings were en vogue in the world of haute couture. The classic black and Latinx New York style was now the property of rich white girls around the world. Field took credit for putting nameplate jewelry on the map. Soon, other designers, from Balenciaga to Céline, would start selling them in high-end department stores like Neiman Marcus and Saks Fifth Avenue, and online retailers were popping up.

I was in the middle of a fashion war over bamboo earrings.

No one really knows who originated bamboo earrings and other styles of doorknockers. The reality is that the first ones were probably produced super cheap somewhere in Asia and distributed through the Asian-American flea market system and to kiosks and open-air markets like the ones I was shopping at in Harlem. And girls from the hood were drawn to their flashy style among all the other low-price-point goods. When hip hop stars like MC Lyte, Roxanne Shanté, and Salt-N-Pepa started rocking these everyday black girl styles in their music videos, they gave the earrings cultural currency. Hip hop touted gold as a luxury material, especially before the bling-bling diamond era of the early 2000s. Salt-N-Pepa even rapped in

"Shake Your Thang": "on my ears, neck, and fingers is crazy gold." The cheap, gold-plated, Asian-store doorknockers could approximate that feel.

Once they became cool, the high-end designers could make that jewelry in real 14K gold and add monetary value to something that was already rich in cultural capital—and their high-end clientele wanted both. But still, no one owned bamboo earrings in the 80s. Upscale versions existed, but designers weren't really trying to stake a claim, and the style remained mostly popular in our black and brown communities. They were also big with the drag queens and nonbinary femme dancers of New York's underground ballroom scene, whose style genius injected a lot of the drama and performativity and gritty queer glam into hip hop style (and they still haven't received the credit they deserve for doing so).

Now, when Patricia Field dressed Carrie in a nameplate necklace and matching earrings, *that* staked a designer and cultural claim to the style in a whole new way. And Field capitalized like crazy. She started selling custom-made nameplate necklaces on her website, noting that they were "made famous" by Patricia Field for *Sex and the City*. Field is a legendary designer for a reason. She took from cis and trans black girl and nonbinary femme cultures when she decided to dress Sarah Jessica Parker's Carrie in these 80s hip hop classics. Field has admitted that she saw young street kids wearing what white people were calling the "ghetto gold" look outside her storefront in the early 90s, and that prompted her to give Carrie her nameplate necklace as a symbol of her single, carefree days as a young girl coming of age in Lower Manhattan. The bling served as a sartorial prequel of sorts to Carrie's *Sex and the City* life. Field's style choices helped elevate Sarah Jessica Parker to fashion icon status, a symbol of everything fashion-forward, edgy, and hip. So here were white women now flocking to designer boutiques and high-end department stores to get the looks that black girls like Shan and I had been dogged out for wearing. On us, to outsiders, the earrings were tasteless, cheap, sleazy even. But once a white woman like Patricia Field said it was fashion, the ghetto gold look was now a vintage something to emulate.

I wasn't aware of this culture war as I deliberated over my choices at the kiosk. My friends and I loved Carrie and the girls. We had weekly *Sex and the City* viewing parties in college, cramming into the apartment of someone with an HBO subscription. Many of my friends considered themselves Carries: leading ladies who were fashionable and down to earth. I was becoming more of a Miranda/Samantha blend: a straight-talking, sexually confident realist, with career goals and a touch of Miranda's quirky girl insecurities. We were all influenced by the fashion on the show. But no one was running around campus wearing a pink tutu just because Carrie wore one or clamoring to buy a nameplate because Carrie sported one. Shan, on the other hand, being at the epicenter, was keenly aware of the conflicted feelings people were having seeing these white stars make a "thing" out of our styles— stealing our culture and distorting its history— and as she explained it to me I instantly understood.

These specific debates might not have hit my Indiana fashion scene yet, but the larger issue was one that was all too familiar. In my black feminism classes in college, my African American woman professor called it "everything but the burden," or this idea that white women wanted the hairstyles and fashion created by and for black women and femmes, they wanted our full lips and thick booties, they wanted to fuck black men, but they didn't want any of the pain and trauma that came with being a black woman. I recognized this dynamic long before my professor gave me language to describe it.

I can't pinpoint the exact moment when I first realized it, but by the time I was in high school, it was a regular conversation among my friends and me: "White girls want to steal everything from us!" It became even more glaring in college once I learned the theory of cultural appropriation in one of my Africana studies courses. After that, I would look around my lily-white campus, seeing white girls mouthing the lyrics to rap songs, tying bandannas around their stringy hair, wearing big hoop earrings and dark liner around their lips, and pushing up on brothas in the club, all while ignoring the black girls, as if we were completely invisible.

I hated this dynamic that the institutional culture seemed to support: black culture was better on white women. And I hated even more the feeling it conjured up in me, that sense of self-doubt, the feeling that white girls were better than me, the belief that black was inferior. Those feelings had taken root in my mind so early in life, and I had worked hard over the years to shake them. As a budding adult, I hated that a white girl could stir them in me still. Every day on campus became a struggle to assert my blackness in the fiercest ways possible, to reclaim my sense of self in a space that was quietly telling me that I was irrelevant. It made me long for the days at Clark Atlanta.

Shan and I went back and forth discussing how black girls had *been* rockin' bamboo earrings and nameplate necklaces, sharing our own stories about the black 80s, comparing and contrasting our experiences. I got my nameplate necklace at Fort Wayne's annual summer Black Expo in the late 80s—the height of the nameplate era. Well, it really wasn't a nameplate; it was gold wire that one of the jewelry vendors shaped into the letters of my name, with a peridot, my birthstone, dangling from the *s*. He was capitalizing on the craze for personalized jewelry by using his pliers to make your name magically appear in front of you. Mom and I each got our own. Mom also had him make a wire that said "Bitch," which he affixed to a faux-leather wristband.

I wore my necklace every day for the next several months. I was thrilled to be a part of the nameplate trend, but more than that, I felt a sense of pride in having something with my name on it. And that's what nameplates did for us: they were a way to claim a sense of self, to claim a space for yourself, to love on yourself, to affirm something that made you uniquely you (even if there were several Tanishas, Keishas, Tamikas, and Shanikas at your school). This especially felt good for girls like me with -isha and -ika names, names our dashiki parents had given to us with pride but the world had told us were ghetto names that would keep us from getting jobs. The nameplates allowed us to wear our multisyllabic monikers with honor. This was something Shandrica and I automatically shared.

Shan, growing up in Bed-Stuy, Brooklyn, had different memories. "They were getting *snatched*!" Shandrica said in her thick Brooklyn accent. "Snatched? Out yo' ears?!" I asked in disbelief. Yes, folks were straight-up robbing girls of their bamboo earrings. It was that deep. Back in Indiana, of course, folks were snatching nameplate necklaces, 14mm herringbone chains, and dookie chains. But to snatch a pair (or in this case two pairs) of earrings out of somebody's ears seemed especially gully to my Indiana mindset. So you had to carry yourself with a kind of boldness that said "Hell yeah I'm fly, and I dare you to try and snatch my shit," Shan explained. Those earrings and nameplates were an investment. You had to have enough dough to buy them. And then you also had to be willing to make the trek to Fulton Street in Downtown Brooklyn, to one of the jewelry/sneaker/leather coat/mixtape all-in-one stores to buy them. I mean, most folk just stuck to the local neighborhood shops, like Tom, Dick & Harry's, to buy their wares. To go all the way downtown—for tha culture—was a sign of your commitment to hip hop fashion. At the store, you'd pick out your favorite doorknockers. There would be no price tag on them, only a label with a code. The clerk then put your earrings on a scale to weigh them. Then they calculated the weight and the value of the gold, which I guess was cryptically registered on the code, and told you how much you owed. I was in awe of Shan's stories as we walked through the sun-drenched streets of Manhattan. We both agreed that no damn white girl was willing to sacrifice alladat for some earrings. Everything but the burden.

After a day on the emotional battlefield of bamboo earrings, the plan was that we were gonna hook up with some of Shandrica's homegirls to hit NYC at night. My only stipulation was that we go to a club I would have heard of in a rap song so that when I was bragging to my hometown friends, I could say, "Yeah I went to X club. You know, the one so-and-so rapped about in that one song?" So as we dressed for the evening, and Shandrica announced that we would go to Club Cheetah, I started rapping, in my best Jay-Z voice, *"From, Club Cheetah to Club Amnesia, The Peanuts in LA, Bubblin' in Dublin."* Yes! (We also planned our next night's adventure: to Halo Lounge in the West Village, a cozy spot with comfy lounge chairs and a small dance floor that Puffy name-checked in the "Welcome to Atlanta" remix and Foxy Brown in "Stylin'.")

I kept singing the "I Just Wanna Love U" lyrics over and over as I applied my tiny bit of makeup with the skills of a novice. Back then, I was into having my eye shadow match my top and shoes. I applied a thick layer of a dusty-rose-colored CoverGirl eye shadow with the cheap applicator that came in the case and some pitch-black mascara that came in a pink-and-green tube, followed by some MAC Oh Baby lip gloss. I slipped on my bell-bottom jeans, unaware of how much I would regret wearing the zip-back pants after I had consumed a couple of drinks. At the moment, I loved those pants because they were on-trend hip-huggers with a nice distressed wash that paired well with my flowy top and the overall vintage boho look I was going for. I put on a pair of massive doorknocker hoops that looked good with my braided updo and slid my freshly manicured pink toes into my pink sandals. I'd found those sandals at a Wal-Mart one night in college when I was looking for shoes to match this cute multicolored sheath dress I bought from Express. They were probably the most stylish thing Wal-Mart had to offer. The whole outfit was slightly homey, but it was acceptable for a pseudo-fashionista from Indiana on her first trip to the Big Apple.

Shandrica's friend Shonda and one of Shonda's homeboys met us at a soul food fusion spot for dinner before the club. This joint was leading the wave of "elevating" soul food to a fine-dining experience. Back at home, our soul food spots were small carryout places that served baked mac and cheese, dressing, greens, fried chicken, cornbread, and black-eyed peas. Wasn't nothing fancy about it, but it was good Alabama-style eating. I was gonna have to get used to this pretentious soul food and the cocktails that offered a shiny Manhattan spin on down-south references: Jook Joint Punch, Harlem Moonshine, Peach Cobbler Cooler.

I hadn't been to many nightclubs, but Cheetah wasn't much different than Cyber Club, the main nightspot for twentysomethings in Fort Wayne. Except for the music. The music here was *way* better. Back home we mostly stuck to the R&B and hip hop tracks popular in the early 2000s, songs by Missy, Nas, Nelly, Destiny's Child, and Ludacris. Occasionally, the DJ would do a little old-school session and play Kris Kross, Bobby Brown, MC Breed, Keith Sweat, and Slick Rick; the music we grooved to at the skating rink before we were old enough to get into the club. Shandrica and them in New York, on the other hand, had been sneaking into the clubs since they were fourteen or fifteen, listening to house and soca and dancehall in addition to hip hop and R&B. The music here was rich and diasporic, showing the range of drums that connects all African-derived music. I was in the big city. I loved it. I loved to dance. I was *killin'* it on the dance floor. And Shandrica bought us all a round to toast me, the birthday girl.

"What is this?" I asked Shan. "Stoli Orange," she said. I nodded and said, "Ah, okay," like I knew what she was talking about. Not that I was aware, but this was back when flavored vodkas were first becoming a thing and Stoli and Smirnoff were changing the game. I wasn't much of a drinker; up to that point, I had only slow-sipped on the universal starter drink: amaretto sour. It was the only thing I knew how to order in a club. And, in all honesty, I had no idea what amaretto was or what made it sour. I also didn't know what Stoli was and figured it must be the type of liquor (not the brand). Whatever it was, this drink had a kick. I quickly felt the light-headedness I'd felt once before: at a Kappa house party in college. Non-drinker that I was, one minute I was hanging back, smashing on some of the fruit out of the Kappa punch. Twenty minutes later I was kicking off my knee-high boots and droppin' it low on the carpeted dance floor, feeling super open and carefree. One of my sorority sisters asked if I was buzzed. I hadn't even had anything to drink! I told her. All I'd had was a cup of the fruit. "From the Kappa punch?!" She looked at me like I was an idiot. "GIRL! The fruit soaks up all the alcohol."

Now it was that same carefree feeling buoying me on the dance floor at Cheetah as I was sweating and pumping and gyrating and attempting mad footwork in my high heels. And the DJ kept playing this song with an infectious beat. "*Just gimme the liiiiight*," the rapper belted in a thick Jamaican accent. "Who is this?" I asked after hearing the song two or three times that night. Sean Paul, Shan said. Then the hook came on again and she and I broke into the butterfly and the pepper seed, dances she'd first taught me in boarding school when we were listening to Li'l Vicious's "Nika" and "Freaks" and Louchie Lou and Michie One's "Rich Girl." By the fall after my trip, Sean Paul's music had trickled out to the Midwest and was on steady repeat on the local hip hop station. "Gimme the Light" was almost an oldie but goodie to the NYC club regulars by then. But on this summer night, it felt brand new, and I got to whining and deep knee-bending every time the DJ spun it.

And Shandrica kept the drinks coming. She was being a good host, shelling out all her new Wall Street *ends* to keep her girl plied with exotic-flavored vodka concoctions. I confided in the guy that was with us that I had never had this much alcohol before when he got a little concerned after I started stumbling on the dance floor. He was crushing on me at that point and was exhibiting the kind of care that surpassed what you'd show to a typical stranger. I accepted his kindness, especially because guys at home were rarely this thoughtful.

He told me to drink plenty of water and update Shandrica. But, not wanting to look like a square, I took one more drink, this time a Stoli Vanilla. And this decision brought me to my bleary self-encounter in the club bathroom mirror.

It kind of went downhill when we left the club and got back into Shonda's car, and I started drunk dialing exes on my baby blue Nokia and alternating between laughing and crying uncontrollably. Which is when Shandrica got wise to the fact that I couldn't "hold my likka," as my mom and her friends would say. According to Mom and her crew, everyone hated going out with that friend who couldn't drink and still keep herself together and presentable. I had become her. Shandrica had been drinking since the early days of college and knew her limits. In Fort Wayne, I had been labeled "fast," but here in New York, it was clear I was anything but. They had a drunk one on their hands! This also seemed to be a scenario they knew how to handle. Shan politely took my phone from me, telling me I'd thank her later. Before I dozed off I apologized for getting too drunk, and slurrily thanked Shan for always being an amazing friend—just like some kind of cliché drunk white girl would do in the movies. She said, "Girl please! It's your birthday." That's right, it *was* my birthday. And the next night, we did it again. But this time, I managed not to get stumbling drunk. I figured out my limit. I got my life in the land of bamboo earrings.

9

Afro Puff

*A*n Afro puff saved my life. I know it sounds cliché to say that I found myself when I went natural. Yet it's the truth. But it wasn't immediate. I walked into a salon in Fort Wayne one day in early fall 2002 and had the stylist, Zetta, who had been doing my hair since high school, buzz the relaxer I'd been growing out over the few months since I crossed the stage at my graduation ceremony at Indiana University in Bloomington. I walked out of the salon without the veil of feminine beauty that I'd never realized until that moment had felt so comforting. I stroked my scalp. It had never been this bare and exposed before. In my teeny-weeny Afro coiffed into tiny coils colored a rich cinnamon brown, I didn't instantly feel beautiful. I didn't instantly love myself. My cheeks felt cherubic and plump, my features too front and center, with nowhere to hide. In the mirror, I thought I looked a bit more masculine than I wanted to feel, or project. I'd always had a tomboy fly streak, but now I wasn't no tomboy playing in the femme buttermilk. I looked like a straight-up boy. Later, I'd come to love wearing my hair buzzed, but in this moment, the only positive I saw was that my head shape was cuter and not as flat in the back as I'd thought it would be. I quickly made an appointment with my favorite braider, Adrienne, and had her grip as many of my short strands as she could grab and braid them into a sea of cascading micro-braids, like the ones she had done for me the summer I went to Myrtle Beach. Protection. Again. I kept those braids in for a couple of months, until I could grow some length and educate myself on how to do my new *natural* hair.

Before social media, it had been a long time since there'd been a national conversation about being natural and what that meant and what it entailed. When I did my big chop, we didn't yet have that social media–ready language. There were no splashy before-and-after Instagram posts to make. There was no *team* with its own hashtag to join or large public Twitter conversation to follow. Then, and even back in the early Black Is Beautiful days before I was born, discussions were regional and local. In the early 2000s they were held on closed email threads, Yahoo! message boards, and locally organized meet-ups. Mostly it was black women forming bonds with other natural women in their workplaces, churches, and gyms so they could steal off to quietly ask each other one-on-one, "Girl, what products do you use?" or "How did you get your hair in that style?"

My little factory town had very few natural women in it—but it was a club that included my mother, who, in true dashiki style, had been natural most of my life. She became my natural hair guru. She stressed the importance of keeping my Sahara Desert–dry hair moisturized at all costs and shared with me her go-to hair care products: essential oils, aloe vera gel, shea butter. I clung to her, and my nascent natural hair journey started to restore the bond between us that had been fractured when I was in middle school and basically decided to run away to a New England boarding school rather than live under my mother's roof anymore. Had I had access to the public natural hair community of today, I would've turned to the YouTube vloggers for help instead. I wonder now how our relationship would have gone without this opportunity to share experiences.

Mom felt our bond strengthening too. I never knew it, because she let me make my own choices, but she was tired of watching me grow up through my many unnatural hair phases: my elementary school Wave Nouveau, the weave ponytails that I set on rollers and baked in the microwave to create Shirley Temple curls in high school, the long Beyoncé weaves in college, and all while making monthly appointments to have "creamy crack," relaxer, applied to my scalp. She kept quiet, but inside, she was waiting for the day that I would be bold enough to try a natural, to push back against the beauty standards that had told me my hair as it grows out of my scalp was ugly, to be black and proud the way that she was as a teenager in 1968—the height of the Black Power movement—when she'd chopped off her hair. I'd never seen my mother wear any hairstyle that conformed to black or white beauty standards, both of which championed long and straight or wet-and-wavy hair. Now, as I felt the wind on my scalp and stared at my suddenly prominent face in the mirror, I was starting to understand just how courageous and unapologetic Mom had to be in the 1980s and 90s in order to wear her hair natural in our perm-addicted city.

In Indiana most women still wore their hair relaxed. If you went natural, people were quick to try to pin down *what kind* of woman you were to account for why you'd want to undergo such a drastic change in hairstyling. Problem was, they had very limited reference points. Every natural woman was either an Angela, an Erykah, or a Kelis. Angela Davis types (this was how folks saw Mom) were militant and politically radical. Angelas didn't take no shit and preferred the most assertive of natural styles: the large halo Afro of the 1960s or a *butch* flattop—both styles my mom had rocked. Erykah Badu types were the artsy earth mothers who styled out in dreadlocks, intricate cornrowed looks or, sometimes, halo Afros. Erykahs wrote spoken-word poems, practiced Buddhism, and wore patchouli and other oils purchased from African vendors. And Kelis types, they were just like the singer: each one a funky wild child, artistic like the Erykahs, but punkier than those earth mothers. They were the most experimental, willing to try different hair colors and combine the different natural styles of the day, like doing cornrows to the back on the left side and leaving the rest in a puffy twist out.

Natural-haired women in Indiana felt like we had to fit these *types* in order to be legible, to be understood by our family and peers. I talked about this a lot with my college sorority sister Kate, who also had a natural mom. Kate and I first had "the talk" about going natural one day during our senior year of college. We were sitting in the apartment Kate shared with her sister, who was a couple years behind us in school. Kate said, almost in a whisper, "I'm thinking about going natural." "I've been thinking about it too!" I confessed loudly, happy that someone else was considering doing this extremely transgressive act. We hugged, awkwardly, an act that solidified our bond and commitment to go through this journey together. Strength in numbers, we figured. Kate had already started growing her hair out, concealing her new growth with braids and sew-in weaves. I had started my transition too, but I caved as graduation approached. I couldn't afford to get my hair braided and the thought of crossing the stage with months of new growth on top of relaxed ends shamed me into getting one last relaxer. Here we were now, after graduation, both natural and both feeling like it wasn't quite what we'd expected.

Being natural came with a steep learning curve as to what the hell we were supposed to do with our kinky mops. It doesn't feel like freedom at first when you have to accept that your natural hair actually takes more time and care than relaxed hair. But watching people try to type you and dealing with the deluge of *whys* and *hows* and *what's it likes* was the hard part. Kate and I would call each other up to vent and laugh about our encounters. Neither of us were Angelas, Erykahs, or Kelises. We were grateful for the blueprints that the neo-soul movement had offered. We were wearing the clothes, listening to the music, speaking the politics. And it was a thrill to see natural-haired women like Erykah Badu, Jill Scott, and India.Arie—women of different hues and body shapes and sizes—rocking vivid prints, oversize earrings, and neutral tones in their music videos and on the pages of *Ebony* and *Essence*. They helped make a space for us where we could feel a bit more comfortable going natural. But we didn't want to *be* these women. We wanted to be ourselves . . . whoever those selves were. We quietly told ourselves we were a part of a special group of brave, independent-thinking women in order to soothe our discomfort and not renege on our decision and run back to the safety of the creamy crack.

But whatever we told ourselves, people in our small Indiana communities needed to see us a certain way in order for our hair choices to make sense to them. Black men especially felt like they had the right to weigh in on our hair choices. I remember being in Indianapolis once, and this black guy walked up to me and said, "Oh, you're going for the African look!," pleased with himself that he had me figured out. It was overwhelming, having to deal with the weight of everyone else's expectations of me and my hair when I was still trying to figure it out for myself. I could see their eyes assessing me as they determined if they thought I was still attractive, still date-able with *nappy* hair. But never seeming to ask themselves if *I* would want *them*. Some black men were all for it; they started calling me "sista" and "queen." In their minds these were honorifics that acknowledged my willingness to buck the norm. For them, my hair choice made me *deep* like Erykah and *confident* like Angela. Somehow, I was better, more authentic than the black women who were still rockin' relaxers. For other men, I was nothing but a Kelis, a man hater. On the hook of Kelis's first hit song, about a cheating boyfriend, "Caught Out There," she shouts, "*I hate you so much right now!*" In the music video, a crowd of women march with picket signs as they chant the breakup battle cry. So, for some black men a natural hairstyle conjured the fear that you hated brothas. Maybe you'd become a lesbian. Others thought my natural hair was an indication (and perhaps even an *invitation*) that I was a freak, sexually open and willing to try anything in the bedroom. Over the years, my mother had become immune to such assumptions and speculations. I was still getting used to it all and was frankly disgusted by the basicness of black men.

I tried on Angela and Erykah and Kelis that first year on my journey to discover who I was as a natural woman. I bought all of the bohemian-looking pieces that Charlotte Russe and the other mall stores in Fort Wayne could offer up. I would even travel down to Indy to visit Kate at the boutique she was working at part time while she finished her student teaching assignment. They had way more clothing options suitable for a naturalista. I walked in one day and Kate was in full-on goddess mode, some sort of Erykah/Kelis hybrid. She had her thick, medium brown hair in what she called a "puff" with a colorful scarf tied around it. I loved it. To create a puff, Kate explained, you wet your hair, apply your favorite moisturizer, pick out your hair, and then take a large hair tie and place it at the base of your hairline and slowly slide it up to gather your hair into a regal Afro puff at the crown of your head. Then you can tie a pretty scarf around the puff to accentuate the look. Kate complemented her puff with an ensemble fit for the Brooklyn bohéme: a billowy top with a floral bohemian print and a cute skirt in a neutral tone. She was wearing makeup, something she never did in college, in earthy tones, and large hoop earrings. She was gorgeous. Clearly, she was making good use of her employee discount. I didn't have the length yet to explore these options, but I was envious. I continued to style my locks in the coil twists Zetta had shown me the day she cut my hair. I still hadn't settled into my natural *look*.

And then I moved to Madison, Wisconsin, for graduate school and everything changed. Deep in dairy country, I found myself and my crew of sisters—most natural, some not—who walked the journey with me. Madison was isolating in an odd new way. I felt my black womanness at every moment. I would walk down the college town's streets and feel invisible; people would not speak to me or do courteous things like hold the door. Yet also, like a musty smell, my identity lingered in the all-white spaces I dared venture into.

In a space like this, you realize how important girlfriends are. I had always been a girl's girl. But in Madison, my girlfriends were key to my social survival. We would frequent lounges with names like Kimia and Crave, ten or twelve black women busting in like a mob, adding a little melanin to the crowd. One night, I looked around the dance floor: all of the white men were with white women and all of the black men were with white women too. In my new crew we'd joke that no one in Madison wanted a black woman but other black women. As sisters, we would dance together, party together, share dreams and goals together, some even shared romantic and sexual love together. We created our own interior world. It was like I used to do when I was a young girl, after my parents' divorce. Back then, I would retreat into myself, manifesting a rich inner thought life and a world of creativity that I didn't share with others. That's what my new friends and I did now. We created a safe space for ourselves where we loved on and validated each other.

My core crew consisted of three other women: Phylicia, Nana, and Cher. I was the newbie on the block; the others had been there for at least a year. I was bold and witty and opinionated but still emotionally fragile and finding myself. It was just like me to make friends with folks who were older or further along in our grad program.

Phylicia, the girl from small-town Georgia, was the diva of the crew. She was also a dedicated activist and historian of the Black Freedom movement. She wore spiked heels in bright colors, halter tops that showcased her large breasts, and skintight pants wrapped with chain belts. She wore her hair natural, often in an Afro puff that accented her high cheekbones, but she also played with straight-haired wigs. She was the first person I'd met who didn't think wearing a straight wig was blasphemous for a natural woman. Phylicia wasn't committed to some ironclad identity just because she had abandoned a perm; she was fun and flirty in her approach to dress and hairstyling.

Nana was a brilliant academic prodigy, taking after her African American mother, a very regal-looking professor at an HBCU in North Carolina. She had a global perspective, one that centered on Africa: her father was Ghanaian, and she had spent her formative years growing up in Nigeria. Always the consummate Afropolitan professional, Nana was far more conservative than the rest of us when it came to dress and hairstyling. She skipped the sweatshirts and halter tops, preferring blouses and blazers, which she would eclectically pair with pieces of printed cloth or handbags, bracelets, and earrings from Ghana. She was also the only one in the crew who still had relaxed hair, a point we never chided her about. But when she would return from her father's homeland, she'd have these beautiful braids that we all envied.

I felt most connected to Cher, the sporty-funky Jamaican-Canadian girl from Toronto a few years older than me. Cher was a

204 · DRESSED IN DREAMS

Leo, like me. We had an instant connection. She was so self-possessed and chill, like I aspired to be. I wasn't all the way there yet, but I at least knew who I was trying to grow into. Cher was very adventurous with her clothing, though she kept her color palettes rather simple: gray (her fave), black, and cream. She would wear funky Kangols and fedoras and military caps to give her bland color palette some edge. She also loved playful shoes and rings. Cher had spent her summers as a college student in New York City, and still saw the city as the place where she went school shopping. She had thick, jet-black hair that she'd pull into twin Afro puffs that sat perched at the sides of the crown of her head. No doubt Cher's athletic sense of sexy had some qualities that made it feel familiar, like Mom's. It was easy for me to trust her taste.

Our group bonding started over nail polish nights. Everyone had to bring their stash of polishes and we would all share and trade and mix and match. But as we played with slick nail paints with names like "Provocative" and "Strawberry Margarita," we chatted about everything from politics to pop culture to hair and beauty. During one of our polish parties, Cher told the group that she had been using this product called Carol's Daughter on her hair. Cher loved Carol's Daughter, mostly because she appreciated the story behind the products.

Lisa Price, the brand's founder, was a woman who loved fragrances. In the early 1990s she was making these body butters and perfumes to use personally and to sell at local festivals and such in Brooklyn. The butters were an instant hit, particularly among all her mom's friends, who would say to each other, "Oh girl, you smell so good! What are you wearing?" "Oh this," one of the others would reply, "Carol's daughter made it." So when Lisa decided to launch a modest mail-order company in 1993, naming it Carol's Daughter was the obvious choice—being Carol's daughter was at the core of her identity. She experimented in her kitchen and added shampoos and hair elixirs to her line. Lisa was a modern-day Madam C. J. Walker, shipping her plain-labeled bottles of magic creams and pomades to women in the tristate area and beyond as word spread. Another wave of the natural hair movement was revving up in the mid-90s, in part in response to the Jheri curl backlash, and also rooted in the black creative energy that was fueling the music, film, and fashion of the Cross Colours baggy jeans era. And Lisa was there to service this small but growing generation of young naturalistas.

After hearing Lisa's story, Cher quickly placed an order, and she had been building her stash of Carol's Daughter products ever since. Cher relayed Carol's Daughter's origin story to us like she was a paid spokesperson for the brand. I was in a hair desert, being so new to wearing my hair natural—I didn't know what the product terrain looked like. I was hungry to try new *magic* potions brewed up in natural hair apothecaries. The name Carol's Daughter sounded trustworthy to me. In it I heard rich legacies that connected black women and daughters across generations. The products were ancestral nostalgia in a bottle. I could relate to being a black woman's daughter—and to being *known* as my mother's daughter. Cher had me about ready to drop a chunk of my grad student stipend on Carol's Daughter.

First, I needed to do some additional research on the brand for myself. That research amounted to asking my bestie Shandrica in New York City what she had heard. Shandrica was in marketing and knew everything about what was happening in the black hair-care world in NYC, on account that she too was going natural. "Oh, yes,

Carol's Daughter is *hot* here," Shandrica told me. The products were particularly popular among young, professional natural sistas in Brooklyn, where Lisa Price had opened her first Carol's Daughter storefront in 1999. The store was in Fort Greene, the heart of the Brooklyn bohéme scene, where black creatives (filmmakers, artists, musicians, writers, and models) lived and worked. Many of them were women with tightly coiled hair, who found that a lot of the mainstream products, even with quality ingredients, still had too much water in them, which meant they didn't properly saturate or seal dense hair. For these women, Carol's Daughter was a lifesaver. Lisa didn't have much in the way of a marketing budget to hire celebrities or models as spokeswomen. Her packaging was super simple to keep her overhead down, kind of like the plain black-and-white labels I used to see on the generic food in the grocery store when I was a kid. So, in the image Shandrica laid out for me over the phone, the women of the Brooklyn bohéme scene became the unofficial face of Carol's Daughter. Cocoa-skinned, conscious Angelas and Erykahs and Kelises and Indias were using Carol's Daughter's Tui Oil and Hair Milk and Almond Cookie Body Butter. It all sounded like something straight out of one of the Spike Lee movies I'd watched as a kid (in fact, Spike and the women he cast in his films were mainstays in the Brooklyn arts scene). I could just imagine Nola Darling sensually massaging Carol's Daughter creme into her short tresses.

It was probably not only women with tight coils who bought the brand, but the narrative of Carol's Daughter was that this was a product *for* us——for black women who had grown up hearing that our hair was problematic, unruly, nappy, and ugly. We had pushed back against all of those negative labels, and Carol's Daughter was the product to help us bring out the best qualities of our kinky hair. With Carol's Daughter, we could shine and feel beautiful.

As loyal customers, we felt betrayed and abandoned in 2011 when Carol's Daughter, under the guidance of music mogul and business-man Steve Stoute, led the now national brand into some "poly-ethnic" campaign. It celebrated the light-skinned, mixed-race, loosely curled hair of women like supermodel Selita Ebanks, R&B singer Cassie, and bohemian soul child Solange (who eventually distanced herself from the campaign). The kinky-haired brown women who had been opening up their wallets for nearly two decades to support Lisa Price were now being cast aside so that Carol's Daughter could compete with brands like Mixed Chicks, Kinky-Curly, and Miss Jessie's that catered to (fair-skinned, multiracial) women with a looser curl pattern. This reignited a texture war. Kinky-haired black women were again being tacitly told that our tight curls weren't desirable and that the aspirational hair was the loose Afro of a woman like Tracee Ellis Ross—the now-beloved biracial daughter of legendary diva Diana Ross, who was then on the popular TV show *Girlfriends*. Products like Miss Jessie's Curly Pudding and Kinky-Curly's Original Curling Custard were designed to elongate our curls to mimic the wash-and-go styles of the so-called mixed chicks. The Afro went overnight from being a style identified by its kinky Q-tip shape to one with looser curls falling in a long, plush bob.

I was deep into my natural hair journey by the time all this went down, rocking honey-blond dreadlocks and watching this texture war from the sidelines. To me, it felt like what I called the "Jayne Kennedy moment" of the 70s, which sparked the rise of the Jheri curl, all over again. Only now I wasn't clamoring to have "good" wash-and-go hair like I was when I was ten. I had a more discerning, critical eye, and to me it seemed like biracial (looking) girls had whined that there weren't any products for them, and the industry capitulated (again), making it all for them.

But back in 2003, when Cher first put me onto Carol's Daughter, it was the kinky-haired chocolate women who were the unofficial face of Carol's Daughter. And right about then, Lisa scored a reported $10 million investment from folks like Jay-Z, Jada Pinkett Smith, and Mary J. Blige. With this infusion of cash, the product packaging and marketing became more sophisticated. By 2005, Jada and Mary had become the face of the line and were the centerpieces of a stunning ad campaign that featured Jada—who had been known for her extremely short cut—with a mop of long, thick ringlets and her bare skin glowing, sitting before a vanity covered with a host of Carol's Daughter products. Mary's ads showed her luxuriating in a bathtub filled with white flowers. I was ready to join the Carol's Daughter diaspora.

And I paid a grip to do so. At home in Fort Wayne, I had been using whatever my mother had in her cabinets or the cheap Suave and VO5 products that, according to one of the message boards I had joined, were good for natural hair. But here in Madison, where I was supposedly *stepping up* my natural hair game, I was now buying products FUBU style: for black women by black women. When my first shipment of Carol's Daughter arrived in the mail, I realized that being natural was also going to be expensive as hell! I paid the price partly for the bragging rights. Just like with fashion, having the hottest hair products before everyone else got *put on* meant that you were cool and style-forward. At the time, I figured Carol's Daughter products used some secret ingredients that no other line used, natural products that made them worth the price. But more than that, using them connected me to the Carol's Daughter diaspora, women across the country who were hearing about Carol's Daughter and purchasing its goods. To be a part of this tribe was especially critical in dairy country, where I felt isolated.

Still, I couldn't afford to live off Carol's Daughter alone: I used those products spaaaar-ing-ly! Only after I had the style down, tested and true, would I use my Carol's Daughter. I did my experimenting and supplemented my hair-care routine with the cheaper products I could find at any Wal-Mart or Target. Some folks thought using white products on my natural hair was egregious. But my grad student budget was real. So I borrowed the "high/low" principle from the fashion world (the idea that you can have one designer piece and pair it with ready-to-wear garments at a much cheaper price point), and I applied it to my hair-care regimen: I used Carol's Daughter finishing products, Tui Oil and Hair Milk, an inexpensive V05 moisturizing shampoo, and a midpriced Biosilk or Aveda deep conditioner—my logic being that conditioners and styling agents were more important than shampoo.

With my new product arsenal, I began exploring different styles, sometimes spending my entire Saturday fussing with my hair. In truth, there weren't that many styles to choose from. We hadn't yet seen the expansion of the faux natural hair market. There wasn't an extensive natural wig market, or kinky clip-in extensions, special kinky braiding hair for Marley twists, or crochet braid Afros. Maybe celebrities had access to those things to give their styles extra flair (Erykah Badu was known to sport faux dreadlocks), but most of the black women I encountered in Madison either wore their natural under braids of the micro or cornrow variety or in single-strand or two-strand twists. Some occasionally did a twist out, but most just wore their hair in a puff. So, I found myself just rotating through this handful of styles that made up the local naturalista ecosystem.

The puff was the easiest look to pull off, and I was overjoyed when my hair was finally long enough to gather into one. It saved me hours in styling time. In the morning I would simply dampen my hair in the shower, allowing it to plump up and stretch a bit before I doused it with Hair Milk and slid my brown hair tie up around the baseline like Kate had shown me, being careful not to catch the hairs in the hair tie as I slipped it toward my crown. If I had some old two-strand twists that were ready to come down, I'd just gather them for a puff, extending time between wash days. Once I had a nice amount of length, I started being a bit more adventurous with my two-strand twists, setting them on rods to make little Shirley Temple curls. I loved my twists. They were easy to maintain and offered a mix of Afropolitan professional and black girl nostalgia, remembering my younger self, before the chemical treatments, in my plaits and beads. On occasion, I would rock a twist out, which is basically just a tex-tured Afro, the crinkles from the twists making it more en vogue and less threatening than an Angela Davis halo Afro.

But I still didn't have my *look* together. I was still holding on to the Angela, Erykah, and Kelis boxes that I'd become attached to, for better or for worse, in Indiana. The black women in Madison were convincing me that there were indeed more options. But I wasn't yet sure what felt most natural *for me*. Stephanie, one of my new friends, helped me solve one of my issues when she showed me the light about my clothes. In Myrtle Beach, I had realized that my hot pants weren't really that hot, and I saw myself in the somewhat con-servative, athletically sexy model of dress that had been handed down to me from my mother. But I didn't see at the time that there was a larger issue around how I saw my body in the American sizing system with all of its inconsistencies and silent acts of shaming. Stephanie made it very clear to me: I was wearing clothes that just didn't fit. I guess I could have gone on that way, but when everything else in my life was coming into sharper focus, it only made sense that my clothes did too.

Stephanie was the epitome of a crunk southern belle: she liked her music full of bass, her outfits prissy, and her hair in a roller wrap. She was a grad student in counseling psychology and a member of my sorority. One day Stephanie and I were shopping at one of the local malls. Shopping together was one of the go-to get-to-know-you activities that black women did together. It was like, if our shopping habits are compatible, maybe we can be friends. Well, Stephanie and I were out on our first friend date and rummaging through the Limited, the young, upwardly mobile girl's mall playground. Stephanie was an opinionated shopper. Time after time as I waved an item I'd grabbed from the rack and did that show-and-tell about what I liked or didn't, Stephanie would weigh in. She'd shoot down or approve my choice as if I was her personal shopper, pulling looks for *her* to wear. But then she started swapping out my picks for the same garments in smaller sizes. "Go try these on," Stephanie pushed. Skeptically I did, and I emerged feeling like a new woman.

Stephanie also introduced me to the concept of having my clothes altered because off-the-rack clothes rarely fit anyone perfectly. A fashionista, Stephanie counseled, had to have a seamstress on call. I nodded demurely as I collected and paid for my new garments: a denim blazer with camel-colored stitching, a short-sleeve knit top with a white faux collar and cuffs and thick chartreuse and teal stripes, and a camel-colored V-neck sweater with a chocolate-brown and burnt orange argyle pattern. I could mix and match these separates, dressing them up and down as desired. Stephanie gave me a satisfied I-told-you-so look of approval. I have to give it to her, when she showed me that I was wearing clothes that didn't really fit me, she revolutionized my style life.

Cher also helped me find my look. "I don't need to own a lot of clothes," Cher pronounced. "If you're really stylish, you can mix and match just a few pieces and make them look different every time." I always liked hanging out at Cher's place, a small one-bedroom that displayed her comfortable aesthetics. The decorations weren't anything overtly *African* or *black* necessarily, but her space always had a super-melanated feel. Over in one corner was a stack of magazines. Cher was an avid collector of fashion mags, one of the few black women I knew who had subscriptions to fashion and lifestyle magazines other than *Ebony* and *Essence*, or hip hop bibles *Vibe* and *Honey*. One of her favorites was *Lucky* magazine. Launched in 2000, *Lucky* was designed to be the go-to magazine for the young (broke) professional woman with a penchant for online shopping, which was a growing trend in the early 2000s. Cher liked that it was focused on shopping and not celebrity gossip and such. *Lucky* was good about showing you one set of garments and then giving you five different ways to coordinate those pieces.

She picked the top magazine off the pile and started flipping through it as we began our usual banter about the latest episodes of *Oprah* and *The View*. Here and there, Cher would interject with a "What do you think, T?," showing me an ensemble to comment on. She'd pull a colored sticker off of an adhesive sheet in the middle of the magazine and place it next to the look she'd just asked me about.

"What's that?" I had to ask after I'd seen her do it a couple of times. She ripped the page out of the magazine and handed it to me. It was a sheet of stickers in the shades of L'Oreal lip colors with either "YES!" or "MAYBE?" printed on them. The magazine encouraged readers to use the stickers like we used multicolored sticky tabs in grad school to mark the garments you eventually wanted to purchase (and of course *Lucky* told you where to go and how much you'd need to spend). I was hooked as soon as I saw those stickers. *Lucky* was my kind of magazine.

Cher also put me onto *Teen Vogue*, saying it was much more accessible than the pretentious "big" or "grown-up" *Vogue*, with its haute couture garments at severe price points. I initially balked at Cher's affinity for *Teen Vogue* because at twenty-four I was still consciously trying to divorce myself from anything *teen*, to assert my grown womanness. But she was right, the looks in *Teen Vogue* were things that I could imagine buying from my favorite haunts. Urban Outfitters, which counted as edgy for me at the time, became one of my new favorite spots. I would tear through the Burlington Coat Factory and Marshalls, both of which always had designer finds. I developed an obsession with Kenneth Cole and Via Spiga shoes and Willi Smith skirts. Our local shoe boutique Sole Man was my new paradise. The shoes were very expensive for my budget, but I'd indulge a couple of times per year. I got my own subscriptions to *Lucky* and *Teen Vogue*, and I would use my finds to do my version of the looks I saw in the magazines.

Now, Cher and I knew that we looked nothing like the skinny white girls in those magazines, who faked joy as they jumped awkwardly and held pigeon-toed postures. But our choice to collect these magazines wasn't really about buying into the mainstream fashion industry's shit. It was about having enough social and cultural capital to hang at its fringes, controlling our engagement, reading the definitions of *fashion* and *on trend* that they offered and disrupting them. Oddly enough, these magazines were my way of staying connected to my black hood girl arts-and-crafts roots, to the days when we made magic out of Dollar General t-shirts and puffy paints. We might have been right next to bougie now, but Cher and I were still masters of the remix. We would take a conventional look out of *Lucky* and discuss ways to blacken and funk that look up. We would sometimes bring our stickered magazines along as we debated the cultural significance of Oprah and Beyoncé or the latest Toni Morrison novel we were reading in an African American literature course.

I can't deny that there was a pleasure and a sense of "I've made it" that came along with these days. I had inched closer to something that felt like my destiny. Inside the alienation of Madison, I'd finally found my home, my comfort place, among a crew of the brightest black women in the country, women who were fashionable and brilliant and creative and well traveled. I was moving socially and culturally into the world of the black literati, and I could feel my life changing. I had traded my relaxer for a natural, my Mike's Hard Lemonade for French red wines, and "yours truly" for "my best" in my email sign-offs.

But I kept hearing: Don't *lose* yourself. Stay *grounded*. And never ever *forget* where you come from. Those are the lessons that black women headed for professional success in the "white man's world" are inundated with. Let an auntie feel like you done become a little too Miss Anne for your own good and she'd put you in your place in a heartbeat. So black women like me were caught between trying to grab ahold of what our new lives and experiences were teaching and offering us without losing those essential bits that anchored us to the communities that birthed us. At times, the pressure was intense because it was a message being reiterated not only in our neighborhoods but all over popular culture and through Tyler Perry's preachy films (the first of which, *Diary of a Mad Black Woman*, came out the year I finished my master's): successful (bougie) black women ain't gon' neva find real happiness.

But through my fashion, I could keep ahold of my black girl self, and that was crucial too. I liked earthy and pastel tones, but I also reveled in vibrant color palettes. I loved blazers in odd colors or uncommon textiles, tailored pants with interesting pinstriped designs, military-style jackets in khaki and camel, denim jackets in every cut. Unexpected pairings. I would never wear a blazer with trousers; instead, I'd wear it over a fitted tee and a pair of tapered sweatpants. Big hoop or wooden or beaded earrings and small odd-shaped handbags complemented my looks. I appreciated the classic lines of tailored menswear, but I also loved odd, funky silhouettes and so-called ethnic prints and patterns. And I loved statement shoes and boots. Once, at Sole Man, I found a fly pair of Carlos Santana shoes. The famed guitarist decided to dabble in the shoe game, and his shoes were as innovative as his music. This particular pair were camel T-strap sandals with a wooden stiletto heel. The toe was slightly open and colored strips of red, pink, baby blue, lime-green, and orange leather crossed the toe and the ankle. I was no longer an Angela or an Erykah or a Kelis. My *own* style was emerging: classy-ethno-funky. That was me.

Everyone in our tightknit crew and on the periphery was drafting off of each other's energy. That's what happens when you're living in a small enclave. It's hard to ever pinpoint who originated a look. But here, unlike other places I'd lived, there didn't seem to be competition to be the one with the latest thing that no one else had yet—that competition that defined my mom's ethos. It was a very hip hop mentality, my mom's. It was all about having and flaunting that thing so that everyone knew they weren't on your level; you were unfuckwitable. She would have been the illest battle rapper. But the women at the University of Wisconsin who had become my friends nurtured each other and treated fashion as a creative outlet. Cher never questioned when I started rocking my two-strand twists in two high buns like hers. Perhaps she adopted the old adage "imitation is the highest form of flattery," or maybe she didn't even notice.

In this world that was now my home, style was a fine art. And for the first time in my life, I considered myself a style architect. That confidence came in part from not being afraid to filter my style through my own lived experience. My hair, my dress was a narrative. It told a story of my journey.

It was only then that I realized just how much I had bought into every narrative about Indiana, not only the ones we had for ourselves, which were deeply engrained, but also the tropes that I saw in outsiders' reactions: that we were inconsequential, that no one knew where Indiana was on the map, that no one wanted to visit. I had accepted this rejection and I was carrying the weight of it around with me. My feelings of inadequacy and dejection were manifesting themselves on my body: believing that being from Indiana meant that I had to show up dressed like a stereotypical Indiana girl, that a coastal city identity came with room to play and create, but the definition of an Indiana girl was quiet and unassuming, narrow and uninteresting . . . and a terrible dresser to boot. That wasn't my truth. In my journey with Cher, Phylicia, and Nana, I learned that I was actually an interesting person, with a cosmopolitan worldview (even though I had never even traveled abroad) and a valid ability to perform cultural criticism. In the words of Jesse Jackson: I am—somebody.

Graduate school was an important time for me too, because it's when I first started seeing a therapist, and I finally shared my personal demons and worked through a lot of things with my mom. I came face-to-face with my own flaws and shortcomings as a mother and learned how to show up emotionally for my son. And this healthier me started to grow out of my head. I was able to see and tackle the self-doubt that had always shadowed my bold, charismatic, rebellious side. It wasn't really about ditching straightening agents and weaves. It was about purging so much negativity and brokenness to get to a truer, lighter sense of self. That was indeed one thing I had gleaned from my days as a pupil in the school of Erykah: "pack light." The external changes I was making were an extension of the deep emotional work I was doing; bringing my outside and inside aspects into harmony. And I was surrounded by a community of black women that I felt more comfortable with than any sister circle I had ever been a part of. So, while it may sound cliché to say, an Afro puff saved my life.

10

Hoodie

I called my mother, resting my Samsung phone in the crook of my neck as I laced up my tan Polo boots. "I'm heading out to a protest," I said. "I just wanted to let you know, just in case I get arrested." She fired back, telling me I needed to keep my ass in the house. I was a bit shocked by her response. Mom had been a dashiki-wearing black feminist freedom fighter in her day! Here I was protesting so that another Trayvon Martin, Islan Nettles, Aiyana Jones, or Michael Brown, or her *own* grandson wouldn't be snuffed out by a vigilante or a police officer. She told me she loved me before getting off the phone. I could hear the concern in her voice. She may have been a lifelong activist, but in this instant she was Tanisha's mama, and her instinct to protect me overrode her commitment to justice. I had texted my dad a similar message, and he'd simply said, "Okay. Have fun," or some such, his way of saying "you're grown, I trust you." I pulled my gray hoodie over my dark skullcap and headed out from Brooklyn to Union Square, where I was meeting up with a group of other activists.

It was November 25, 2014, the day after a grand jury had voted not to indict Ferguson police officer Darren Wilson for the murder of unarmed teenager Michael Brown. We'd all been watching the proceedings for weeks. The searing pain and rage and collective action in Ferguson was on every screen and streaming on social media timelines viewed from our smartphones. Local Ferguson activists, most of them years younger than me, had been putting their bodies on the line daily, facing down tear-gas bombs and police in riot gear. And many of us felt for them, and for ourselves, and for our children, and our emotions manifested in a wall of solidarity against injustice that aligned black and brown communities across America, and the world really. And the decision on Wilson came two days after twelve-year-old Tamir Rice was gunned down by Cleveland police officers who said that they'd believed he was an adult brandishing a gun at people in a local park. Turns out, he was carrying an airsoft gun, clearly marked with an orange tip to identify it as a toy. But within two seconds of arriving on the scene, the officers shot Rice. He died in the hospital the following day.

I thought of my own son, who was now a 6'3" college student.

But even back when he was Tamir's age, he towered over adults. I always feared that white folks would read him as older than his years . . . and dangerous, which would always make him a suspect, never ever a possible victim. And the truth was, that fear never went away. I still knew that any of these slain kids could have been my kid. My Malik.

They could kill any of us—adults, children—with impunity. We couldn't even get a murderer indicted! That police badge protected them from any consequence, no matter how blatant and documented their crime. City to city, the shared experience boiled up and lifted people out of their safety zones to protest in the streets, to stand and assert that *this was clear injustice*. The collective *we* that was ready to fight back was huge. History was not going to gaslight us on this. We rallied behind the cry "Black Lives Matter," a declaration and political ideology given to us, in hashtag form, by three black queer women, seasoned activist-organizers Patrisse Cullors, Alicia Garza, and Opal Tometi.

In New York City, the first big protest after the Department of Justice announcement on Wilson was to be on November 25. Several chapters of #BlackLivesMatter and various student prison abolition and LGBTQIA activist groups did the organizing. I had participated in other #BlackLivesMatter and women's rights marches in the city. I had even co-organized a Free Marissa Alexander rally when I lived in Massachusetts. But the mood in the air was far different this night. All of us who participated saw that we had to do something major to send a message to our government that we wouldn't just stand by and bear witness to the murder of black folks, then watch silently as their killers went untried and unpunished. How could we even live if the very people who were charged with protecting us knew they could kill us and the state wouldn't do a thing? This was terror. And the human response was rage.

I've always had a brazen personality. I had learned to temper it once I became a working professional. Not now. I felt that familiar unleashed feeling that I get when I've decided to lower my inhibitions. I would be reckless tonight. I knew it. And I'm sure my mom did too. Something was compelling me out into the frigid cold. I walked toward the subway. My cell phone started buzzing. I looked down to see "Mom" on the screen. I answered. She said, "I'm sorry for telling you not to go to the protest. You gotta go fight for what you believe in. You be safe, and you call me if you get arrested. I got a little bit of money to bail you out." I told her I loved her, again. And with Mom's blessing, I headed to downtown Manhattan to go fuck shit up.

That energy kept rising up. It was a long ride out of my borough and across the bridge, so I got to sit with it awhile. And I realized that I was channeling this feeling into productive activist energy, fighting for a just cause. But the raw energy was one I'd felt before. I could remember a time when I had used it against the very black girls I was now fighting to protect. It was this memory—more than that of the list of names of slain black people on those now-popular "&" t-shirts—that gripped me on this train ride.

I was walking home with Monica, one of the new friends I'd made after Mom and I moved into McMillen Park. Monica was a sweet, frail-boned, amber-brown-complexioned girl who wore huge, thick, plastic-framed glasses; they kinda looked like Cazals but way less fly. Her sweet, slightly nasal voice made her sound kind even when she was saying something sassy. She had short, thin hair, which she often wore in a half-up, half-down style, though the "down" part didn't touch beyond the back of her hairline. She looked up to me, it was clear, so ours was an easy friendship on account that I loved being the boss. It had been chilly earlier in the day, but now the sun was out, so Monica had removed the black zip-up hoodie she'd been wearing and was carrying it on her arm. She was so proud of that damn hoodie. Wasn't nothing special about it. It was just a well-worn piece of outerwear that was too big for her in the first place. We made the right turn from Werling Drive onto Billington Court, Monica's street. I don't even remember what we were talking about, but suddenly I snatched the hoodie off Monica's arm and started running with it, darting and juking, like the boys did when we played tag. Monica couldn't catch me.

"Give it back, Tanisha," she whined. Toying with her was fun. I was like a cat with a mouse. I started putting on the jacket and teasing her about wearing the oversize hoodie: "Why you wearing this big ol' hoodie anyway? It don't even go with your outfit!" Then I saw the huge dumpster at the end of the court coming up, I darted over and put the jacket through the window-size hole as if I was gonna drop it in. Monica came running up beside me on those weak legs. Winded, she gasped pleadingly, "Give it baaaack! Tanisha, that's my mom's boyfriend's jacket." Undaunted, I kept swinging the jacket, no real plan for how to end my cruel taunting and ended up throwing it in, half accidentally and half intentionally.

Monica started crying. She had to get that jacket out of the dumpster or else face a whoopin' by her mom, or worse, her mom's boyfriend. She climbed up into the dumpster. Instead of helping, I just kept taunting, making fun of her for getting in with the trash, blocking her exit route. I picked up a large stick and used it to flick bits of the garbage at her as she made for the precious hoodie at the far end. The court was eerily empty of kids that day. If the older girls Aquilla and Yvette had been outside I never would've thrown Monica's jacket away like it was an empty take-out box. I mean, they teased Monica too. Hell, getting teased and pushed and cracked on were just part of the culture. But even I knew this was over the top, unacceptable. It was an abuse of power that wouldn't garner me any street cred in the hood.

As it dawned on me, I got scared. Not because of the beatdown that might come if Monica told the older kids. I was scared of myself. Why was I doing this to my friend? The one who loved my mother, the brave D.A.R.E. officer who came to her classroom each week to try to protect her from the dangers of drugs. I was watching myself do this, seeing an utterly evil streak that, at ten years old, I didn't even know I had. So eventually I threw the stick down and moved out of the way. Monica climbed out of the hole, hoodie in hand, covered in tears and sniffling, her body hunched over as she cradled the hoodie and walked toward her house. I didn't apologize or even beg her not to tell her parents. I just walked the rest of the way home in silent shame.

Monica's mom never came to my door asking me why I'd terrorized her daughter. No older kids jumped me for abusing Monica. Monica didn't mention it the next day at school. That made the punishment even worse. God knew. God had seen what I'd done to my friend. And like the deaconesses at my church taught us in Sunday school: God don't like ugly. I punished myself for the next twenty years for what I'd done to Monica.

Most of us encounter that ugly power inside us at some time or other. I still don't know why this was the day when it came out in me. I do know why the hoodie was so important to us—to Monica, its protector, to me, the bully. That hoodie was everything for a girl who had very little. She had been charged with caring for that hoodie. That responsibility to care for someone else's garment doesn't just come with a threat if you mess up, it comes with the pride of knowing that someone trusted you enough to care for their belongings. To be seen as reliable and dependable—loyalty—was key to our street code. Also, it is warm and comforting inside a hoodie—it's a garment that can change the emotional tenor of your day—and someone she looked up to had given her that experience. She probably liked wearing the oversize jacket that represented the protection we all wanted from a male figure in our mostly women-headed households.

Perhaps I was jealous because my parents had just split up and my dad was now living across town. Perhaps I wanted to punish Monica for having a man in her home; I was too young to recognize the havoc of misdirected emotions. Maybe I was projecting that kind of brutal heartlessness because I thought I needed it to survive life in the projects. I don't know. Monica and I graduated from the same high school, in the same class. I had years and years to apologize. But merely thinking about what had happened was too painful. I never did.

Here I am now, well into my thirties, getting ready to march through the streets of New York City in *my* hoodie. Trayvon Martin's murder had made the hoodie the national symbol for racial profiling. A black male or masculine-presenting person, of any age, wearing a hoodie (a garment pretty much universally popular among all age groups, mind you) had to be a thug, and any white person would be justifiably frightened by the sight, the narrative went. It was absurd reasoning. It was obscene. And it was familiar. And it was everywhere. Everyone from black and brown folk of the hip hop generation to white kids wanting to show solidarity to black congresspeople wore hoodies in protest. Its symbolism was universally recognizable in that moment.

I couldn't let my failures as a child stop me from helping my people now, from showing up for my son. But this memory also put me in touch with a wellspring of humility, of questions that are not so easy to answer. When we grow up with such an intense need to defend ourselves, with the imperative to prove that we can survive, where's that line between being tough and becoming an abuser? How do we cradle the honor that comes with protecting those in our community, especially the weaker and lesser-resourced among us, even while allowing ourselves to be fully human, flawed and imperfect?

And encasing this mystery that I faced at ten is an adult, abstract layer of the same problem. If you're black, you are already so vulnerable that letting down your guard is unthinkable. Black folk in America are marked out by the most normal things. Wear a hoodie, you're a criminal. Carry a toy, you're a threat. Wear big earrings, you're making us uncomfortable. You are told all your life that your hair is wrong, your culture is primitive, your family is broken, your mind will never be bright enough for college, your money will never be good enough to buy luxury. And as for your aspirations to be treated with basic human decency and allowed to prove your merits for yourself, let alone maybe exercise specific legal rights as a citizen—well, it's a crapshoot whether that will be met with total

silence or murderous fury. You're constantly fighting just to be perceived as acceptable in the most basic of situations.

Here I was, facing my own personal guilt for what I'd done to
Monica. I saw into myself: I didn't walk into that protest in the mindset of a hero. I was a real, flawed person, and I was going to join hundreds and thousands and ultimately millions of real people, some of
whom did think they were heroes, though they were still emotionally broken, some of whom were woke and righteous in the street
but shallow-minded in private, or brave in their defense of black
men but would never stand up for black women or for someone they
read as queer. And still all of us, with all of our character flaws, could
fully acknowledge that what the police were doing, and the courts
were exonerating, and the legislature was ignoring was wrong. Our
movement was imperfect, but it was necessary.

When I got there, a group of activists had already gathered. From
the looks of things—and the shaky style of organization—the
leaders appeared to be college students. In fact, some were even
sporting their black Greek letter organization jackets. Definitely
students.

As more people poured in, we became a strong chain of bodies
striking out of the park and onto the street. It was rush hour in Manhattan. Our leaders had decided—whether on the spot or ahead of
time, I didn't know—that we didn't care. We chanted "Whose
Street? Our Streets!" as we filed our group of hundreds of young
and not-so-young protesters through the grid of cars whose motion
we had stopped completely. We held posters that read "#Fergu-
sonEverywhere" and "No Justice, No Peace." Some people honked

their horns in a show of support, joining us in the chants as we passed their lowered car windows. Others looked exhausted from a long day's work and just wanted to make it home to remove their shoes, relieve the babysitter, and eat dinner. I felt a pang of guilt for interrupting their evening commute. But the names, a few names among the countless, of those who have been brutally murdered—Aiyana, Michael, Tamir, Eric, and more, and more, and more—kept me focused. The cops' guns and clubs and fists and boots had converted these siblings from flesh into a hashtag that would live on in a digital memorial or on a cotton t-shirt or hoodie, like the one I was wearing. Surely their lives were worth the inconvenience.

Police officers followed alongside of us now. I couldn't really tell if they were there for our protection or to club one of us if things got a little too rowdy. It was that feeling of uncertainty that caused a palpable tension between us that night—when you don't know for sure if someone is an enemy or an ally, your instinct for caution pushes you toward enemy.

I had a complicated relationship with the police. I had grown up in a *chosen family* of police officers, after all. I referred to the black women and men from Mom's police academy class as "aunt" and "uncle." I understood the blue code that police officers lived by. My mom had put in 20.5 years (she always made sure to mention that half year) on the force before retiring in 2000, when I was in college. No one was gonna mess with Amye Ford's daughter, not to even give me a speeding ticket. So the Fort Wayne police force

in particular made *me* feel safe in my town. Outside of my personal
safety net, though, black folks were being clubbed upside the head
and put in illegal chokeholds. And I knew I wasn't covered any-
where beyond Fort Wayne. Like most black kids of the hip hop
generation that I knew, I grew up with a distrust of the cops. In
1991, we'd all watched the camcorder video of LAPD officers
repeatedly beating Rodney King with their billy clubs. It played on
loop on our television sets. And N.W.A.'s anthem "Fuck the Police,"
released four years earlier, resurfaced in my mind.

So I lived with the simultaneous love of my mom and Aunt
Debbie and Uncle Fred and my disdain for the white cops who
looked at black folks as inherently criminal. It was an uncomfortable line to toe, and when I first started doing police brutality and
corruption-related activism, I didn't know how to reconcile these
two sentiments. Among activists, I rarely shared that my mother
was a cop. When I did, I made sure to emphasize that she wasn't
one of those sellout, Uncle Tom cops who would harass her own
people rather than fall out of favor with the white cops they pa-
trolled the beat with. I always remember how much we hated the
donut-eating black cop in *Boyz n the Hood* who told Furious (Lau-
rence Fishburne) that he wished he'd killed the burglar who tried to
rob his house because it would be "one less nigga out here in the
streets we'd have to worry about."

Seeing the police detail trailing us didn't deter our group from shout-
ing chants like "No justice, no peace, no racist police!" It was a much
less soulful and tamer version of the popular Black Panther Party

chant from the 60s: "The revolution has come, OFF THE PIGS!" It still felt defiant to chant it directly to the group of cops in navy blue following us through the streets.

I knew the terrain of lower Manhattan only slightly better than I had when I was roaming it with my best friend Shandrica in the early 2000s. I had no real sense of where we were going. I flowed with the crowd, snapping pics and videos and posting them on Twitter, chronicling everything that was happening for my followers while trying not to bump into one of the many cars stuck in the streets we had shut down. We had learned to use social media as an insurgent technology, to break stories and archive the movement because the mainstream news often covered protests unfairly, downplaying police violence and amplifying the actions of protesters. That's if they covered the stories at all. Twitter became the front line of breaking news, the realer, truer source, we believed.

We had been marching for a while when I saw the sign for Franklin D. Roosevelt East River Drive, known as the FDR, and we started winding up the on-ramp. As I rose a little higher in the crowd, I looked around with my phone trying to digitally capture just how large our group had become. I removed my thick gloves and typed, "We've shut down FDR," tweeting a blurry pic of young protesters in hoodies and army-style jackets with their mouths open and signs in their hands. The collective energy of outrage was palpable.

Across the country, people, many in hoodies, were doing similar large-scale acts of civil disobedience. The previous month protesters had shut down the 75/85 interstate in Atlanta to call attention to the brutality in Ferguson. And a few days after our protest, a group of twenty to twenty-five—mostly women and nonbinary femmes—chained themselves to the BART trains in Oakland, halting transportation, as they chanted "Black Lives Matter."

And across the country, people were having this discussion about the face of the movement. We were kids from the hood talking about issues that affected the hood. We would dress like ourselves, reflecting our culture. I was a working professional by this point, Dr. Ford with three degrees behind my name, pretty solidly middle class. But still with the same dashiki spirit I was raised with, still a hood girl from a factory town where nobody loved us, still a black woman with family members living in that same hood, strung out, underemployed, and overpoliced. It was just instinctual for me to pull out a hoodie that night I took the train over to join the younger protesters in Union Square. Donning my hoodie made it clear for me and for onlookers, I hoped, that despite my education or the fact that I "made it out" of the hood, I wasn't making any distinction between myself and my family members or any other black person. What for? I knew my degrees and my newly found middle-class status wouldn't save me, not when it takes a police officer two seconds to decide to shoot.

We started jumping over the cement guardrails on the FDR. It was my turn to jump up and over. I thought for a second about my knees, which were way creakier and more prone to inflammation than those of the young mixed-race group of college-aged kids that surrounded me. But I made it up and over the wall, and my knees handled the impact my Polos made as they hit the concrete. I then hopped over a smaller metal median until I was facing the oncoming traffic.

More chanting and honking from cars. Rush hour traffic was halted for what looked like miles. All I could see were white headlights beaming out in the cold of night. If there was to be one iconic image for the hashtag #FergusonEverywhere, this would be it. Our numbers seemed to grow exponentially, several hundred now. What I didn't realize at the time was that there were other protesters who had taken over other parts of the city—in Times Square, in Brooklyn. The number of officers was increasing too. And they went from passively following us to now forming a blockade and trying to herd us off of the FDR. No one turned back, not even when the officers started yelling into their bullhorns. We just raised our hands and started chanting repeatedly: "Hands up, don't shoot!"

We were at a standstill for nearly an hour—chanting and raising clenched fists—facing down the police. Eventually, the leaders in the front started squeezing through the chain of cars sitting on the FDR, and the rest of the group started to flow in that direction after them. I did too. We weaved right in front of the police who had formed the initial barricade, continuing our ear-piercing chanting as the cops warned "Turn back!" through their bullhorns. Another direct act of defiance. A smaller group of people—mostly young white kids—continued past that barricade and past another. "Where are they going?" I turned to ask a few youngins. "It looks like across the Williamsburg Bridge," someone said. The police had set up a secondary barricade to block the pedestrian entrance, and the group was heading to face it. I knew this was my cue to leave. Those white college students could have a standoff with the police and survive. But I knew that cops had no regard for black lives.

I braced myself as I walked down a steep slab of concrete, once again working through conflicted feelings. Part of me felt like a chump for exiting; another part of me remembered the promise I'd made my mother to return home alive. And to do that, I'd have to find home. I had no clue where I was. My Samsung battery was dead; I had taken so many pictures and videos for Twitter. I tightened the drawstrings on my hoodie to keep the cold out as I walked.

Since the 1930s, people have been wearing thick jackets with hoods to work in warehouses and refrigerated spaces. Truck drivers, construction crews, and sanitation workers wear them as they move in and out of the cold. Because Fort Wayne is such a manual labor city, you could find a hoodie at any discount clothing store, right near the Dickies and Carhartt work clothes.

You could always tell the difference between someone who was wearing a hoodie for utilitarian purposes and those of us who were wearing them for style. The workers in Fort Wayne tended to wear navy or black hoodies, often faded from constant wash and wear, or stained by paint or oil. Us kids wanted our hoodies in bright colors: red, purple, green, turquoise. And the color had to be new, fresh off the rack. If your hoodie got too faded and you continued to wear it, you would get *roasted*: "Look at Larry with that ashy-ass hoodie on!" *Ash* was antithetical to everything black. We wore lotion, cocoa butter, and Vaseline to keep our skin moist. If your skin got dry, got that white ashy cast to it, you'd get clowned. Same thing with our clothes. If your hoodie, or any other garment for that matter, had a similar ashy look from too much washing, it was a source of shame.

Sweatshirts were a staple in our wardrobes, at every age. Athletic wear in general was popular everyday wear when I was a kid, everything from varsity jackets to short sets with team names on them. I remember having a pink Hanes sweatshirt with matching sweatpants that I loved to wear to school in third grade. But hip hop culture helped to make hooded sweatshirts exceptionally popular. Hoodies were more expensive than your basic sweatshirt, and the best ones were made from thicker material, which makes sense if you think about the utilitarian purposes of the hooded sweatshirt. All of the hip hop artists of the 1990s, particularly folks from New York, had a hoodie. As Cross Colours and Karl Kani and African American College Alliance brands became the hot styles worn by our favorite black entertainers, the hoodie became a centerpiece of urban or hip hop fashion.

Every black kid in my town wanted one. To be down, to be a part of the culture, you had to rock a hoodie. They were no longer the work uniforms we'd seen our mamas and daddies and uncles and cousins roll out of bed at the crack of dawn to throw on before a backbreaking fourteen-hour work shift. Hoodies were now status symbols. They symbolized hood wealth and cultural capital. Everybody knew that stick-up kids wore hoodies to commit robberies and that graffiti artists wore them to conceal their identities, and gang members wore them to rep their sets. Not everybody was involved in all of that, but hip hop had cemented elements of the hood aesthetic into broader American culture. Those elements of gang and tagging culture (like intricate fonts and bold color palettes) that we black kids took and emblazoned all over our sweatshirts gave the hoodie a new life. Soon, even white kids were rocking hip hop–styled hoodies.

The garment had transcended its origin as a blue-collar worker's mantle and then as the gear of the underground economy. It had even transcended blackness in many cases—but still, cops didn't revere the hoodie like we did. I remember riding home many nights in high school, seeing cops with some kid in a hoodie handcuffed. That same image, always with black and brown kids, was all over shows like *The Wire*. Black or brown and in a hoodie equaled always already a criminal.

I saw a similar response to the hoodie when Malik and I lived in London. On one hand, London was this posh, cosmopolitan city, with its high street shopping and iconic red double-decker buses. On the other, it was just as racist and xenophobic as any city in the United States. In British public discourse, kids who wore hooded sweatshirts were called "hoodies." It was a coded way of saying that these kids were from poorer boroughs and council estates—government housing akin to US projects. It was also a way to say "immigrant." The face of the hoodie was usually a black or brown kid from an East or North African, British Caribbean, or Middle Eastern nation. Some establishments even enacted hoodie bans, declaring that no one wearing a hoodie could come in. Labeling them by their clothing choices allowed government officials to front as if this wasn't about race or religion or citizenship: it was about a *garment* that *concealed* one's identity. But it was clear to me that the British government was using the same smear tactics as they had used to denigrate Afro-Caribbean youth in the Black Power era. Hoodies were a menace, and the British government wanted them out.

After the police killed a man named Mark Duggan, the *Guardian* plastered images of brown kids in hoodies setting cars on fire. Duggan, a suspected drug dealer and gang member, was shot to death by London police officers in August 2011, less than a year before Trayvon Martin was killed in Florida. Youth (mostly immigrants) across the Tottenham neighborhood of London and in other parts of the United Kingdom began protesting police brutality in what was dubbed by the British media as the "BlackBerry Riots"—on account of the fact that the young activists used their smartphones to coordinate on a national scale. So black and brown youth activists in the United Kingdom and United States shared the hoodie as a common political symbol, one that came straight out of hip hop and British grime culture. Living in both places, I experienced the deep kinship between these overlapping movements against police brutality.

Many of the people who took to social media after Trayvon's murder to post pics of themselves with their hoodies up took to the streets after Michael Brown's assassination. Some had lists of names emblazoned on them linked with the & sign or political messages in short, easily hashtagable words and phrases, like "Assata Taught Me"—reverencing our radical foremother Assata Shakur, who fled persecution in the States, after being falsely imprisoned for killing a cop, for a life in exile in Cuba. She still remains on the FBI Most Wanted Terrorists list. This digital-friendly language was made to live on one of the most hip hop garments. A hip hop protest ethos: quippy rhymes of hip hop music, the political power of the classic protest poster, and the body as a billboard.

Back in the 1960s, when my mother was coming of age, black-owned mail-order companies sold James Brown "Say It Loud, I'm Black and I'm Proud" sweatshirts (without hoods) and t-shirts. The shirts were advertised on the pages of black magazines—from *Ebony* to *Sepia*. Screen printing technology was still rather new then, so the shirts were cutting edge. And others like it began to crop up over the 1970s, shirts with Malcolm X and his famous quotes stamped on them. Shirley Chisholm, the first black woman to run for the Democratic party's presidential nomination, made campaign sweatshirts with her slogan "Unbought & Unbossed" on them. My generation wore "Black Is Beautiful" and "It's a Black Thing, You Wouldn't Understand." We reimagined the Malcolm X t-shirt, this time with a huge X that ran from shoulder to hipbone across the shirt. People today find them online, we bought our shirts in department stores and boutiques that specialized in "urban wear," or we would buy iron-on letters to create our own messages.

At this protest, I'd seen many people wearing "Assata Taught Me" t-shirts designed by Ferguson activist Ashley Yates and others (many of them queer-identified folk) using teespring.com. These designs used simple fonts, an aesthetic throwback to those days when we used to decorate hoodies with iron-on letters. They helped to solidify a font, color palette (usually black hoodies with white lettering), and format for the burgeoning Movement for Black Lives. People were drawn to these retro hoodies with striking political messages like "This Ain't Yo Mama's Civil Rights Movement" and "I'm Not My Grandparents. Signed, These Hands." The protests that began after the murder of Trayvon Martin kicked off an entire market for message tees and hoodies that was largely internet based. By the time Donald Trump was elected president, message hoodies and t-shirts had become a part of mainstream fashion, and conversations about cultural appropriation reached a necessary fever pitch.

I used to roll my eyes when everyone wanted to look like a celebrity when we were in middle school. "So-and-so said I look like [fill-in-the-blank] celebrity." I never thought I looked like anyone famous, which made me hate the whole notion. But then Yo-Yo hit the scene in the early 90s, just as I was heading into puberty. Yo was striking. A protegee of one of my fave rappers, Ice Cube, Yo-Yo was equal parts beautiful and powerful. She had hazel eyes that looked like mine and a similar reddish-brown skin color. Her baby-face features gave her a youthful look, but her brick-house body showed that she was clearly grown. Our birthdays were only two days apart; both Leos. For me, no one made the connection between hip hop and woman-centered black politics better.

The early 90s were big for conscious rap, or rap with a political message. X Clan, Jungle Brothers, A Tribe Called Quest, and De La Soul made us proud of our blackness as they flowed about our African roots and our need to rise up as a community. Jersey's Queen Latifah went for an Afrocentric militancy that was marked by her frequent wearing of Zulu headdresses and kente cloth. She was clearly channeling an African Queen—her stage name and nick-names, such as "Mama Zulu," made this clear. I admired Queen Latifah. She was who I wanted to be . . . when I turned twenty-eight. In my mind then, twenty-eight was the peak grown woman age. But I *loved* Yo-Yo. I wanted to be her *now*. She was just so real to me. Girls in my hood didn't walk around in kente and beads and head wraps. Queen Latifah felt aspirational—but somewhat inaccessible. Yo-Yo, with her regular black girl clothes, looked just like one of us.

Yo-Yo reminded me of the cool, older, streetwise girls I orbited at the skating rink, hoping they'd pull me into their crew. I wanted to join Yo's Intelligent Black Women's Coalition (IBWC) the first time I saw her "Stompin' to the 90s" video. IBWC was a pseudomilitary black girl empowerment group that sometimes made appearances in her videos and was referenced in her lyrics. They carried flags with "IBWC" on them and dressed in matching uniforms: biker shorts and t-shirts. Yo-Yo often sported a black fitted hoodie with "IBWC" on the back.

Yo-Yo was a feminist before I even recognized the word, using her music to help black girls discover their power and speak out about injustices in our community. She did it without being overly preachy. She was the culture, and she was helping us find empowerment through the culture. I mean, my mother had always been one to fight for the equality of women. She believed that women deserved equal pay, that we could do the same jobs as men, and that women shouldn't be bound by traditional gender roles. But Yo-Yo's feminism was cooler to me because it was hip hop. None of us had jobs in middle school, so issues like workplace harassment and equal pay felt like foreign concepts. But listening to a woman rap about us being "black pearls," and how to confront a dude who was talking wild crazy to you at a party, or how to check a hater who was throwin' salt on your name—those were actually useful life skills.

Yo-Yo and the IBWC made everyday black girl games like double dutch and hopscotch look and feel political. They taught my friends and me it was okay for us to claim our flourishing sexuality while demanding respect from boys, and that was so relevant to where we were in life. In her hit song "You Can't Play With My Yo-Yo," she raps, "*Check the booty, yo, it's kinda soft and if you touch you're livin' in a coffin.*" IBWC gave me the space to become womanish as I inched closer to adulthood, and that space allowed for the fun of being a black girl in the hood, choreographing routines for school talent shows; the emerging street style that was becoming synonymous with hip hop; and the passionate consciousness of women's rights issues that my mother espoused.

I went to the crew of fourteen-year-old girls that I ran with and told them that we needed to start calling ourselves IBW: Intelligent Black Women. I mapped out an entire mission statement: we would compete in talent shows and write empowering messages and be leaders and role models to other black girls in our school. I think this was, in part, my attempt at working through what I'd done to Monica four years earlier. I declared that our colors would be red, yellow, and green (colors that looked like the Afrocentric colors of the Ghanaian flag that I had seen in hip hop videos). There were about twelve of us, and we would break down into three subgroups of four; everyone would be responsible for buying a hoodie in their subgroup's color. It had to be a hoodie specifically. Not only because Yo-Yo wore one but because, to me, the hoodie was tantamount to our political message. It got at the heart of black life and the reality that at the core we were fighting to be seen, heard, understood, treated fairly, and not be beaten up by the police.

It didn't surprise me when, in the wake of Trayvon Martin's murder, it was the hoodie, not any of the other garments he was seen wearing in his social media pictures, that became the rallying symbol of the aptly named Million Hoodie March.

I was lost in thought as I made my way to Washington Square Park. Finally, I had found a recognizable landmark. I had been walking for a mile, bracing myself in the cold. I made my way past the park on Waverly Place to Sixth Avenue. I rounded the corner. A block away, on the corner of Sixth Avenue and Eighth Street, I saw familiar red lettering. It was Gray's Papaya, the hot dog joint that Shandrica had taken me to during my first trip to New York City a dozen years earlier. Whenever I thought of Gray's Papaya, I thought of Carrie Bradshaw slammin' on a Gray's dog during an episode of *Sex and the City*. I didn't realize until that moment that I was famished, drained of all of my energy. I dipped into Gray's and bought a dog dressed in ketchup, mustard, and onions. I didn't even eat meat anymore, but I felt a need to connect with something familiar, something that threaded all these versions of me who were relating so differently through time and space to this present moment. I bit into the dog and found a shabby little counter to stand at for a few minutes. The shop wasn't very warm. The constant stream of folks coming in kept a rush of cold air circulating through. I tossed my trash and headed back out into the cold. I looked up at the Sixth Avenue and Eighth Street signs, and chuckled to myself, remembering how confused I had been the first time I came to New York: "But why are there two sets of streets with numbers? How do you know the difference between them?" I'd asked Shan on more than one occasion. But here I was now, something of a New York City dweller, having lived there for almost a year. I made my way back to Brooklyn so I could charge up my phone and let my parents know I had made it home. Alive.

Epilogue

Designer Handbag

I breezed through the door of Louis Vuitton on Fifth Avenue in New York City, doing my best I-belong-here performance. It was a routine I had done in countries around the world for years at this point. But still, the Indiana girl in me was never fully comfortable just *being* in a place. It was as if I had to constantly remind myself that I made sense in a fine restaurant, at an art gallery, or at a dope music festival. Over the years, I had learned to speak a cultural language that made me virtually *unclockable* as a ghetto girl from Hoosier country—but in the midst of new experiences, self-doubt would creep in: They can see right through me. They know I am not *of* this place.

I hadn't had to do this getting into character in quite some time. I had grown comfortable in my life, brushing shoulders with minor celebs, publishing my work in the hottest magazines, "summering" in Europe, and working with some of the most creative artists in the game. But I was still new in New York, and there were days like this. Days when that little voice of the girl with the Wave Nouveau who dreamed of getting out of Fort Wayne, Indiana, but never believed she could would flare up in my belly. So I would go into performance mode to help calm her down. For some reason, the thought of being at a Louis store on Fifth Avenue conjured up those old ghosts, and I was turning into the method actor, living the "I belong here" role.

See, in Indiana, black folk were considered the up-South country 'bamas. Most of our people had actually migrated from Alabama; you can hear it in our southern accents, blending with the pioneer twang of white Indiana folks. But when prejudice causes folks to look at Alabama and see "backward" mentalities and habits, it sees the same in us. So when Beyoncé called herself a "Texas Bama" in "Formation," I felt her. I understood the work of *naming* and *reclaiming* that she was doing. I'm not from the South, but my folks too are considered bumpkins compared to the black folks who migrated from the global south to Los Angeles and New York City. People out east always call me out when they hear the twang in the way I say "any" or "water." I still sound like an Indiana girl, no matter what. And I actually like that, my accent rooting me in a place and community.

And in moments like this trip to the Louis store, I have to peer deep inside and see that sometimes I still put the same kinds of restrictions on myself that I was raised with. I still feel those beliefs about coloring within the lines, to be safe, creep up whenever I do something creative. My art flourishes more when I leave convention behind, but how often does my instinct veer toward obedience and roll past the political power of disobedience? Part of me still thrives on being that good worker bee, that effective cog in the machine. This is my default and I have to actively tug at myself to keep growing. And for the most part, I have, and for that I am proud.

As I walked through the door into Louis Vuitton, I was working through all of these emotions and battling down the creeping impostor syndrome by telling myself that I had the capital to be there, that I was a boss. I guess it wasn't that shocking that, despite whatever amount of funds was in my bank account, I would feel *some type of way* when entering a store that is universally considered the epitome of global luxury.

Black people are regularly racially profiled in these spaces. Eighteen-year-old college student Trayon Christian was arrested for supposed credit card fraud after purchasing a $349 Ferragamo belt at the Barneys store just around the corner from where I was now shopping. No charges were filed, but Christian still had to live with the anger and embarrassment that resulted from the arrest. (He would eventually win his lawsuit against the New York Police Department, receiving a $45,000 settlement.) Dana Hale was accused of credit card fraud at Saks Fifth Avenue in a posh Detroit suburb after purchasing $6,700 worth of Louis Vuitton goods and charging them to her personal business credit card. One of my own friends, Sierra, was recently arrested at a luxury-brand store after another black woman was caught stealing a handbag; the clerks assumed that just because Sierra happened to be in the store at the same time she was the other woman's accomplice. And I mean, if

Queen Oprah could be profiled in Hermès in Paris and at a high-end boutique in Zurich, Switzerland, surely I could be profiled in Louis Vuitton. Of course, I had been in Louis stores before. I did a loop around the flagship Louis store on Les Champs Élysées, the same one Carrie Bradshaw took an embarrassing dive in on the final season of *Sex and the City*. Social conventions were screaming at me that if *Carrie*, the thin, white, blond New Yorker, didn't belong in a Louis store in Paris, clearly my kinky-haired black ass didn't belong there.

However, I was giving my best I-belong tease, wearing a high-waisted, tea-length, A-line skirt that screamed modern take on a fifties starlet and an effortless tank and designer flats. I didn't have an appointment, and my mind was telling me that I was supposed to have one. In my vision, they would serve me champagne (like they did for Carrie when she went to Prada), I would browse in the exclusive enclave that was only for serious buyers. You didn't come to Louis Vuitton on Fifth Avenue to window shop. Thankfully, I wasn't there to window shop. I was actually coming to swap out my small Damier Ebène Neverfull tote for the same size in the *Azur* Canvas. I had never spent that much money on a bag before, and the frugal part of me just wanted to return it altogether, to see the funds reappear in my bank account. But no, I had achieved a major milestone and had decided: *Girl treat yo'self! Do something big and extravagant!* I was gonna stay committed to the plan.

I took a deep breath and then exhaled till I felt my abs hug my rib cage as I breezed through the doors of the house of Louis. *Method acting!* Aaaaaand it was a mad house. Forget about the serene, posh, champagne-sipping environment I had imagined. There were bodies of all races and nationalities and genders moving rapidly through the store, flowing up and down the staircase that led to the second

floor, pawing on the handbags and wallets that were perched strate-
gically, grouped by collection.

I didn't know enough about New York geography to realize that
this Fifth Avenue store was in the heart of a major tourist area, so
there was no way that this store was gonna create an air of exclusiv-
ity. Still, I wasn't chancing it. I was a black woman walking into
their store with a large bag in my hand. I knew I fit the stereotypical description of a booster, a professional thief who nicks
things from high-end stores for "clients" or for herself. In movies,
boosters are almost always black or Latinx cis and trans women.
Meanwhile, white women who steal from high-end stores are labeled
kleptomaniacs, mental illness (and usually a fancy family name) protecting them from doing jail time. Security officers were keeping
an eye on their respective zones while they tried to look intimidating yet inconspicuous. I did the shopping version of "hands up,
don't shoot" by keeping my bag outstretched in front of me in one
hand and my receipt in the other. My actions needed to look delib-
erate, intentional, to quietly signal to the guards that I posed no
threat. I was simply there to conduct business. After all, they
couldn't know that the bag I was carrying held the square chocolate-
colored box encasing my Neverfull tote.

It's a shame that over the years I've come to know this particular
ritual so well. Black women are so often accused of stealing and
writing bad checks at retail stores that you learn these submissive
postures and performances of being a "good shopper" in order to try
to leave with at least a bit of dignity intact. I can remember being in
Big Lots, a discount store, with my mother when I was in grade
school, and she was buying some home décor pieces for our apartment. She whipped out her checkbook and started writing a check.

The clerk asked for her driver's license and then proceeded to write "BF" next to her driver's license number on the check. "What's that?" Mom snapped at the young white girl. Nothing gets past Mom. I looked at the check. My ten-year-old eyes didn't see anything. "Why did you write 'BF'? Does that stand for black female?" Then I started to get what was happening here. The girl explained that it was a new store policy, that they were required to write the race and gender of everyone who pays with a check. Having been profiled in stores and followed around for the better part of her life, Mom wasn't going for it. And in her best Miss Sophia from *The Color Purple* voice, she told the girl, "I am a police officer, and I know this is a discriminatory practice. Get your manager." Mom had the power of her shield to stand on, but most of us do not. So most of us play the part of Good Shopper to avoid a confrontation. And that was certainly my choice today, especially since I had on my good Dorothy Dandridge skirt.

I was snapped out of character by an older Chinese man in a suit who was saying something in his native tongue in a loud and pushy tone to one of the store employees, an Asian woman who looked to be in her late forties. The veteran clerk told the man in a firm voice, in English, "I'm Japanese, not Chinese," and then she glared at him before rolling her eyes. I could feel that. I could see in her body language how sick she was of wealthy overseas businessmen coming into the store and talking to her like they had no regard for women, all while misidentifying her nationality. I liked her. She'd probably be happy to help me after that unpleasant encounter. "Excuse me," I said. She turned to me and flashed what New Yorkers would consider a warm smile but back home would register as indifference. She had an old-school, elegant pageboy haircut, was dressed conservatively in a dark color, and had a small Louis Vuitton crossbody bag in the signature monogram neatly draped across her torso. I explained to her that I was looking to exchange my current Neverfull for the *azur* one. To make a long story short, I ended up walking out of that store with the same *ebène* bag but in a larger size and a crossbody bag like the clerk's for my mother. I left chuckling to myself: that New York hustle. She got me to spend *more* money.

As I headed back to the train, I started thinking about my mother and the knockoff Louis Vuitton bag she used to carry back in the day. It came back with her from a visit to Aunt Brenda in LA. When they were together, you knew they were gonna shop. And their asses weren't above shopping at the Crenshaw swap meet to buy knockoffs and deeply discounted wares. Of course, Mom could buy a knockoff bag from the flea market back home, but she was on the hunt for something special.

Back in Fort Wayne, they sold the absolute cheapest knockoffs. My bestie Shandrica had one rule when it came to knockoffs: in order to pass a knockoff, you've got to know what the real thing looks like. Most folks in Fort Wayne did *not* know what a real Louis looked like. As a result, they were rockin' bags that were so knocked off they didn't even look like they were in the same family as the original. The very best of our flea market bags looked like hard plastic blocks with the letters pressed on in cheap-looking metallic gold. A Crenshaw market knockoff was way different than these Fort Wayne pretenders. The LA stalls were known for getting the good knockoffs, bags that were supposedly made in the exact same factories as the originals, bags that you had to be a knockoff whisperer to *clock*.

Mom found this *bad* Louis Vuitton bag. I'm talking *cold*. It was designed like a vintage medical bag. Boxy in shape, it had two tiny handles on top and metal, rectangular boning, which allowed the bag to sit wide open like a fully extended mouth. It was actually the dream design for a hoarder. You could see everything in your bag at once without having to dig your hand around feeling for the desired item. The light brown Louis Vuitton leather went around the top of the bag. The rest was covered in the classic LV canvas. I remember when she showed it to me. I couldn't believe we had a Louis in the house! The only time I'd ever seen Louis Vuitton gear was in hip hop videos. I didn't know it at the time, but the threads my favorite rappers were sportin' were Dapper Dan designs that were technically knockoffs—even though he was a legit designer who was making doper wares than the real European houses were—because he brought the Louis Vuitton material from a textile market on Delancey Street in Manhattan's Lower East Side.

I opened the bag for the first time and saw that the craftsmanship of this knockoff extended to its very lining. I rubbed my hands against the smooth suede, feeling my hand hit each of the bag's four 90-degree angles. It also had a long crossbody strap, which I slung over my shoulder as I began prancing around our living room. I had plans for this bag. I was already angling on how I could convince Mom to let me carry it to school.

I can picture the bag in my mind's eye now and, looking back, that treasure definitely had that Dapper Dan quality. It was not the type of thing Louis was making at the time, but it was exactly the kind of design that black and Latinx folk would love. It was so original, largely because it had that vintage feel. It referenced a time period long passed. It was a bold centerpiece, something you built your whole outfit around. And it's no wonder that my mother, the clotheshorse who liked conversation starters, would be drawn to that bag.

My mother is a natural leader. But, much like me, or perhaps I'm much like her, she doesn't actually like to draw a lot of attention to herself. She's not much inclined to "perform" for a crowd—*except* when it comes to clothes and accessories. She was *that chick* when it came to edgy hairstyles, clothes, and bags. Mom wanted people in our community to see her as a style maven. She'd always been that way. And she encoded her brazen sense of style into my DNA, though I didn't realize the extent to which her confidence and bravado would present itself in my adult life. So of course Mom had to parade her new "Louis" around to her friends first. She wore it to all sorts of occasions—from work events to girls' night at their favorite local restaurant. I kept asking to wear it, and doing little things to claim it as my own like saying, "Ooh, look how this would match my outfit, Mommy!" or "Dang, I can't wait for Laura and Ranotta to see me in *our* bag." Like it was this piece of communal property. Eventually, Mom got tired of her latest bauble, and it was my turn to sport the Louis doctor bag at school.

And when I did, I had so many tales about where the bag came from and what Louis was as a brand. It was my turn to be the teacher. I had been to LA after all. I, too, had my mother's penchant for style. And I was naturally bossy. So I held court about my new Louis bag. It was a good enough knockoff to impress my mom's friends, so of course it could pass for some twelve-year-old girls who had never left Indiana. Even my cousin Nikia, who knew all things "hot," "boosted," and "knocked off," thought this bag was a good Louis replica. And I kinda still didn't all the way understand what a knockoff was anyway, so I thought it was like a junior Louis or a Louis cousin or something. I wore that bag until I destroyed the lining. I literally ripped it from the sides. It was still a pretty good-quality bag, and I figured it still cost a lot of money and that Mom would be pissed. But she wasn't. Not even a little bit. She didn't even fuss. It was a toy. An inexpensive amusement that had done its work. It had garnered the oohs and ahhs that she was looking for, her delight in revealing, "Girl, this a knockoff," to which they'd oohed and ahhed more before inspecting the bag for telltale signs that it wasn't authentic.

Here I was, more than twenty years after Mom brought that gorgeous knockoff Louis Vuitton bag home, walking out of the Fifth Avenue New York City store carrying a real Louis of my own. The hip hop part of me felt like, *My nigga, we made it!* I had traveled the world, was now living in Manhattan, and was finally (kinda sorta) making enough loot that I could buy a Louis bag. This was all way more than little girl me from the hood of Fort Wayne, Indiana, could have ever imagined. My father must have felt like this when he went from being a starving kid caught up in the juvenile detention system to purchasing a shiny Rolex with his college-degree-underwritten corporate paycheck.

It wasn't about the material items themselves, it was about the hard-fought journey to financial stability, the feeling of being starved of your desires for most of your life and then finally having the access, finally being able to indulge. This is a feeling that few black folk in this country get to feel. We're far more used to getting punished for even daring to *want*. That reality singed my feeling of accomplishment. At the same time, that truth made my purchases feel transgressive, renegade.

The feminist side of me understood well the perils and trappings of capitalism and the racism inherent in how luxury goods are produced, marketed, and sold. But in that moment, just beyond the Louis store, my innermost primal being delighted in the feeling of enfranchisement—belonging, participating. I had gotten a taste of luxury, even if it did come in the form of a chaotic tourist trap: *this is what it feels like to straight bum rush your way in, to push past the structural barricades, to catch a black girl freedom dream dressed as a handbag.*

The more introspective, emotional part of me thought about how I had become my mother. When I was living in Wisconsin, I started to have a greater appreciation for my mother, for her sacrifices and unconditional love. But now I looked at myself and literally saw her: I dressed like her, walked like her, felt her same commitment to community. I strolled through the streets of New York that day not feeling like a black Carrie Bradshaw; instead, my mind was on my mother and her model of black womanhood. She who taught me so many lessons just by the clothes she wore and the way she styled her hair. I thought about how, as a young girl, I'd mimicked her every move and wanted everything she had. Now, I was a proud dashiki daughter, dressed in my own dreams.

Acknowledgments

I call this book my "oops baby" because I never intended to write her. But now that she's here, I love her dearly and am grateful for everyone who helped nurture her while she was in gestation. Big thank-yous to my parents, Herman and Amye, for letting me comb through their old memories with the excitement of a nosy daughter, not a seasoned researcher. Thank you to my aunt Marcia, who kept me laughing with tales of my mother's childhood. To the rest of my Ford, Perry, and Glover family: I love you fiercely, even though I don't get home as often as I'd like to. My son, Malik, you are my everything. You've given me purpose, kept me moving and fighting for something other than and bigger than myself, and for that, you will always be my favorite person on the planet. Thank you.

I am the result of the eclectic bricolage of events, encounters, and relationships that have animated my life. To the human affectionately known as #paypalbae (lol!), thank you for seeing me and loving me and always encouraging me to be my best. Thank you to every auntie, godmother, big mama, and big cousin who has imprinted on me. I hope you can see your influence on my life as you read this book. To my amazing friend groups, especially my Village Woods homies, my '98 Trues, the Ratchets, Darnell Moore and the Black Brilliance brunch crew, my 19 E.P.I.P.H.A.N.Y. line sisters, my #TeamTextures/#OBC crew, the Black Bean Society, my U-Dub posse, the Easton's Nook writers, and my Radcliffe/Harvard community (especially my housemates/chosen kin Tomashi Jackson, Nia Evans, Cookie, and Cornbread), you make me better; you bring me joy; you keep me lifted.

I tried some new methods for researching this very contemporary book. Thank you to my research assistant, Simone Austin, the digital wiz and curator who tracked down obscure newspaper and magazine articles on dashikis, Cross Colours jeans, and everything in between. You listened intently each week via Skype as I worked through my ideas, sometimes sharing your own, while keeping everything perfectly organized. This book is stronger because of you. Thank you Tiffany Gill, Regina Bradley (who also read early drafts), Aja Burrell Wood, S. D. Lee, Zeke Bryant, Siobhan Carter-David, Terrell Starr, Sherry Johnson, Josie Martin, Cicele Bennett, and others who allowed me to test out this rather unorthodox interview-type thing with them. Your stories helped my own become lucid. And to the boarding-school friends who helped me piece together my fragmented memories of my days in Concord, thank you. You forced me to muster up the courage to look at my fifteen-year-old self and to see her in a more forgiving way. I relied heavily on the social media friends and strangers alike who responded to my random Facebook, Twitter, and Instagram queries that went a little something like: "What did you call this (fill-in-the-blank garment) where you grew up? Did you own one?" These simple posts generated much conversation and really helped me see the regional—and even diasporic—similarities and differences in this thing we call hip hop fashion.

My most sincere thanks to the people who were integral parts of *Dressed in Dreams'* invisible scaffolding—the people behind the scenes who believed in this project and made this thing go. To my fabulous St. Martin's editor, Elisabeth Dyssegaard: You changed my life over a cup of tea in a random Manhattan Le Pain Quotidien! Thank you for being a supportive coach and keen-eyed reader. My agent, Tanya McKinnon, and her colleague Carol Taylor are the baddest in the game. Thank you for being true visionaries and brilliant strategists. Emma Young, the talented developmental editor who helped me let go of my "academic voice" and press for something more alive and sensorial, I am forever indebted to you. You gave me permission to eat, pray, love my way through Paris and then put it all on the page. To my illustrator, Veronica Miller Jamison, you are #blackgirlmagic! You instantly caught my vision and brought lanky, ordinary-girl me to life in fashionable form. Special thank-yous also to those who so generously read early drafts: Akiba Solomon, Treva Lindsey, Jessica Johnson, Brittney Cooper, and Joan Morgan. You all listened to me as I tried to work this thang out, making loving-yet-critical suggestions along the way. Cheers to you! Thank you to my University of Delaware AFRA family—especially Maloba, Tammy Poole, Tiffany Gill, and Gabrielle Foreman—who cheered me on as I wrote and supported my need to take time off to finish this book. Erica Armstrong Dunbar, Martha Jones, and Claude Clegg also provided great mentorship and advice along the way. Thank you also to the countless colleagues who offered models for how this "crossover" thing could be done. To my St. Martin's

team, especially Laura Apperson, Alan Bradshaw, Katie Haigler, DJ
DeSmyter, Brant Janeway, and Sarah Schoof, thank you for being
awesome! Thank you to photographer Darcy Rogers, who shot the
Dressed in Dreams cover image, and MUA Kenya, who did my
makeup (shout out to the team at the MAC store on West 125th
Street in Harlem!). Little did we know when we linked up on the
hottest day of the summer to take some random photos for my
website that we'd create art that would live on a book cover.

Last, to every black girl and non-binary femme living in some
no-name town: I see you, I acknowledge *you*. I hope you see yourself in my story—in our collective story—and realize sooner than
I did that you don't need anyone's permission to dream!

Tanisha C. Ford

Harlem, NYC